ALL OF GRACE

An Earnest Word for Those Who
Are Seeking Salvation by the
Lord Jesus Christ

By

C. H. SPURGEON

MOODY PRESS

CHICAGO

ISBN: 0-8024-0001-9

25 26 27 28 Printing/LC/Year 92 91 90 89

Printed in the United States of America

Contents

1

To You

HE WHO SPOKE and wrote this message will be greatly disappointed if it does not lead many to the Lord Jesus. It is sent forth in childlike dependence upon the power of God the Holy Spirit, to use it in the conversion of millions, if He so pleases. No doubt many poor men and women will take up this little volume, and the Lord will visit them with grace. To answer this end, the very plainest language has been chosen, and many simple expressions have been used. But if those of wealth and rank should glance at this book, the Holy Spirit can impress them also, since that which can be understood by the unlettered is nonetheless attractive to the instructed. Oh that some might read it who will become great winners of souls!

Who knows how many will find their way to peace by what they read here? A more important question for you is this: Will you be one of them?

A certain man placed a fountain by the wayside, and he hung up a cup near to it by a little chain. He was told some time after that a great art critic had found much fault with its design. "But," said he, "do many thirsty persons drink at it?" Then they told him that thousands of poor people, men, women, and children, quenched their thirst at this fountain, and he smiled and said that he was not troubled by the critic's observation. He only hoped that on some sultry summer's day the critic himself might fill the cup and be refreshed and praise the name of the Lord.

Here is my fountain, and here is my cup. Find fault if you wish, but do drink of the water of life. I only care for this. I would rather bless the soul of the poorest street cleaner or rag-gatherer than please a prince and fail to convert him to God.

Do you mean business in reading these pages? If so, we are agreed at the outset; but nothing short of your finding Christ and heaven is the business aimed at here. Oh that we may seek this together! I do so by dedicating this little book with prayer. Will you not join me by looking up to God and asking Him to bless you while you read? Providence has put these pages before you, you have a little spare time in which to read them, and you feel willing to give them your attention. These are good signs. Who knows but that the time of blessing is come for you? At any rate, "The Holy Ghost saith, To day if ye will hear his voice, harden not your hearts" (Heb 3:7-8).

2

What Are We At?

I HEARD A STORY; I think it came from the north country. A minister called upon a poor woman, intending to give her help, for he knew that she was very poor. With his money in his hand, he knocked at the door; but she did not answer. He concluded she was not at home, and went his way. A little later he met her at the church and told her that he had remembered her need: "I called at your house and knocked several times, and I suppose you were not at home, for I had no answer." "At what hour did you call, sir?" "It was about noon." "Oh, dear," she said, "I heard you, sir, and I am so sorry I did not answer, but I thought it was the man calling for the rent." Many poor women know what this meant. Now, it is my desire to be heard, and therefore I want to say that I am not calling for the rent; indeed, it is not the object of this book to ask anything of you, but to tell you that salvation is *all of grace*, which means, free, gratis, for nothing.

Often when we are anxious to win attention, our hearer thinks, "Oh! Now I am going to be told my duty. It is the man calling for that which is due to God, and I am sure I have nothing to pay it with. I

will not be at home." No, this book does not come to
make a demand upon you, but to bring you something.
We are not going to talk about law and duty and punishment, but about love and goodness and forgiveness
and mercy and eternal life. Do not, therefore, act as if
you were not at home; do not turn a deaf ear or a care-
less heart. I am asking nothing of you in the name of
God or man. It is not my intent to make any require-
ment at your hands, but I come in God's name to bring
you a free gift which it shall be to your present and
eternal joy to receive.

Open the door and let my pleadings enter. "Come
now, and let us reason together" (Is 1:18). The Lord
Himself invites you to a conference concerning your
immediate and endless happiness, and He would not
have done this if He did not mean well toward you. Do
not refuse the Lord Jesus who knocks at your door, for
He knocks with a hand which was nailed to the tree for
such as you are. Since His only and sole object is your
good, incline your ear and come to Him. Hearken diligently, and let the good word sink into your soul. It
may be that the hour is come in which you shall enter
upon that new life which is the beginning of heaven.
"Faith cometh by hearing" (Ro 10:17), and reading is
a type of hearing; faith may come to you while you
are reading this book. Why not? O blessed Spirit of
all grace, make it so!

3

God Justifieth the Ungodly

THIS MESSAGE is for you. You will find the text in Romans 4:5, "To him that worketh not, but believeth on him that justifieth the ungodly, his faith is counted for righteousness."

I call your attention to those words, "Him that justifieth the ungodly." They seem to me to be very wonderful words.

Are you not surprised that there should be such an expression as that in the Bible, "That justifieth the ungodly"? I have heard that men that hate the doctrines of the cross bring it as a charge against God, that He saves wicked men and receives to Himself the vilest of the vile. See how this Scripture accepts the charge and plainly states it! By the mouth of His servant Paul, by the inspiration of the Holy Spirit, He takes to Himself the title of "Him that justifieth the ungodly." He makes those just who are unjust, forgives those who deserve no favor. Did you think that salvation was for the good and that God's grace was for the pure and holy who are free from sin? Perhaps you think that if you were excellent, then God would reward you; and maybe you have thought that because you are not worthy, there-

fore there could be no way of your enjoying His favor.
You must be somewhat surprised to read a text like
this: "Him that justifieth the ungodly." I do not wonder that you are surprised; for with all my familiarity
with the great grace of God, I never cease to wonder at
it. It does sound surprising, does it not, that it should
be possible for a holy God to justify an unholy man?
We, according to the natural legality of our hearts, are
always talking about our own goodness and our own
worthiness, and we stubbornly believe that there must
be something in us in order to win the notice of God.
Now, God, who sees through all deceptions, knows that
there is no goodness whatever in us. He says that "there
is none righteous, no, not one" (Ro 3:10). He knows
that "all our righteousnesses are as filthy rags" (Is 64:
6), and, therefore, the Lord Jesus did not come into
the world to look after goodness and righteousness with
him, but to bestow them upon persons who have none
of them. He comes, not because we *are* just, but to
make us so; he justifieth the ungodly.

When a lawyer comes into court, if he is an honest
man, he desires to plead the case of an innocent person
and justify him before the court from the things which
are falsely laid to his charge. It should be the lawyer's
object to justify the innocent person, and he should not
attempt to screen the guilty party. It is not man's right
nor in his power to truly justify the guilty. This is a
miracle reserved for the Lord alone. God, the infinitely
just Sovereign, knows that there is not a just man upon
earth who does good and does not sin. Therefore, in the
infinite sovereignty of His divine nature and in the
splendor of His ineffable love, He undertakes the task,

not so much of justifying the just as of justifying the ungodly. God has devised ways and means of making the ungodly man to stand justly accepted before Him. He has set up a system by which with perfect justice He can treat the guilty as if he had been free from offence; yes, can treat him as if he were wholly free from sin. He justifieth the ungodly.

Jesus Christ came into the world to save *sinners*. It is a very surprising thing, a thing to be marveled at most of all by those who enjoy it. I know that it is to me, even to this day, the greatest wonder that I ever heard of that God should ever justify *me*. I feel myself to be a lump of unworthiness, a mass of corruption, and a heap of sin apart from His almighty love. I know and am fully assured that I am justified by faith which is in Christ Jesus, and I am treated as if I had been perfectly just and made an heir of God and a joint-heir with Christ. And yet, by nature I must take my place among the most sinful. I, who am altogether undeserving, am treated as if I had been deserving. I am loved with as much love as if I had always been godly, whereas before I was ungodly. Who can help being astonished at this? Gratitude for such favor stands dressed in robes of wonder.

Now, while this is very surprising, I want you to notice how available it makes the Gospel to you and to me. If God justifieth the *ungodly*, then He can justify *you*. Is not that the very kind of person that you are? If you are unconverted at this moment, it is a very proper description of you. You have lived without God; you have been the reverse of godly. In one word, you have been and are *ungodly*. Perhaps you have not even

attended a place of worship on Sunday, but have lived
in disregard of God's day and house and Word. This
proves you to have been ungodly. Sadder still, it may
be you have even tried to doubt God's existence and
have gone the length of saying that you did so. You
have lived on this fair earth which is full of the tokens
of God's presence, and all the while you have shut your
eyes to the clear evidences of His power and Godhead.
You have lived as if there were no God. Indeed, you
would have been very pleased if you could have posi-
tively demonstrated to yourself that there was no God
whatever. Possibly you have lived a great many years
in this way so that you are now pretty well settled in
your ways, and yet God is not in any of them. If you
were labeled ungodly, it would describe you as well
as if the sea were to be labeled *salt water.* Would it
not?

Possibly you are a person of another sort. You have
regularly attended to all the outward forms of religion,
and yet you have had no heart in them at all, but have
been really ungodly. Though meeting with the people
of God, you have never met with God for yourself; you
have been in the choir, and yet have not praised the
Lord with your heart. You have lived without any love
to God in your heart, or regard to His commands in
your life. Well, you are just the kind of person to whom
this Gospel is sent, this Gospel which says that God justifieth *the ungodly.* It is very wonderful, but it is happily available for you. It just suits you. Does it not?
How I wish that you would accept it! If you are a
sensible person, you will see the remarkable grace of
God in providing for someone such as you are, and you

will say to yourself, "Justify the ungodly! Why, then, should not I be justified, and justified at once?"

Now, observe further, that it must be so. The salvation of God is for those who do not deserve it and have no preparation for it. It is reasonable that the statement should be put in the Bible, for no others need justifying but those who have no justification of their own. If any of you are perfectly righteous, you want no justifying. You feel that you are doing your duty well, and almost putting heaven under an obligation to you. What do you want with a Saviour or with mercy? What do you want with justification? You will be tired of this book by this time, for it will have no interest to you.

If any of you are giving yourselves such proud airs, listen to me for a little while. You will be lost as sure as you are alive. You righteous men, whose righteousness is all of your own working, are either deceivers or deceived, for the Scripture cannot lie and it says plainly, "There is none righteous, no, not one." In any case, I have no Gospel to preach to the self-righteous, no, not a word. Jesus Christ Himself came not to call the righteous, and I am not going to do what He did not do. If I called you, you would not come; therefore, I will not call you. No, I ask you rather to look at that righteousness of yours till you see what a delusion it is. It is not half so substantial as a cobweb. Be finished with it! Flee from it! Believe that the only persons that can need justification are those who are not just in themselves. They need something to be done for them to make them just before the judgment seat of God. Depend upon it, the Lord only does that which is needful.

Infinite wisdom never attempts that which is unnecessary. Jesus never undertakes that which is superfluous. To make him just who *is* just is no work for God; that were a labor for a fool. But to make him just who is unjust, that is work for infinite love and mercy. To justify the ungodly is a miracle worthy of God, and it is.

Now, look. If there be anywhere in the world a physician who has discovered sure and precious remedies, to whom is that physician sent? To those who are perfectly healthy? I think not. Put him down in a district where there are no sick persons, and he feels that he is not in his place. There is nothing for him to do. "They that are whole have no need of a physician, but they that are sick" (Mk 2:17). Is it not equally clear that the great remedies of grace and redemption are for the sick in soul? They cannot be for the whole, for they cannot be of use to such. If you feel that you are spiritually sick, the Physician has come into the world for you. If you are altogether undone by reason of your sin, you are the very person aimed at in the plan of salvation. I say that the Lord of love had just such as you are in His eye when He arranged the system of grace. Suppose a man of generous spirit were to resolve to forgive all those who were indebted to him; it is clear that this can only apply to those really in his debt. One person owes him a thousand pounds, and another owes him fifty pounds; each one has but to have his bill receipted, and the liability is wiped out. But the most generous person cannot forgive the debts of those who do not owe him anything. It is out of the power of Omnipotence to forgive where there is no sin. Pardon, therefore, cannot be for you who have no sin. Pardon must be for the guilty. Forgiveness must be for the sinful. It would be absurd to talk of forgiving those who do not need forgiveness or pardoning those who have never offended.

Do you think that you must be lost because you are a sinner? This is the reason why you can be saved. Because you realize that you are a sinner, I would encourage you to believe that grace is ordained for such as you. One hymn writer even dared to say:

> A sinner is a sacred thing:
> The Holy Ghost hath made him so.

It is true that Jesus seeks and saves that which is lost. He died and made a real atonement for real sinners. When men are not playing with words or calling themselves "miserable sinners" in false humility, I feel overjoyed to meet with them. I would be glad to talk all night to bona fide sinners. The inn of mercy never closes its doors upon such, neither on weekdays nor on Sunday. Our Lord Jesus did not die for imaginary sins, but His heart's blood was spilled to wash out deep crimson stains which nothing else can remove.

He that is a dirty sinner is the kind of man that Jesus Christ came to make clean. A Gospel preacher on one occasion preached a sermon from, "Now also the axe is laid unto the root of the trees" (Lk 3:9), and he delivered such a sermon that one of his hearers said to him, "One would have thought that you had been preaching to criminals. Your sermon ought to have been delivered in the county jail." "Oh, no," said the good man, "if I were preaching in the county jail, I should not preach from that text, there I should preach 'This is a faithful saying, and worthy of all acceptation,

that Christ Jesus came into the world to save sinners'
(1 Ti 1:15). This is true." The Law is for the self-righteous, to humble their pride; the Gospel is for the lost,
to remove their despair.

If you are not lost, what do you want with a Saviour? Should the shepherd go after those who never
went astray? Why should the woman sweep her house
for the pieces of money that were never out of her
purse? No, the medicine is for the diseased; the quick-
ening is for the dead; the pardon is for the guilty; liber-
ation is for those who are bound; the opening of eyes is
for those who are blind. How can the Saviour and His
death upon the cross and the Gospel of pardon be ac-
counted for unless they be upon the supposition that
men are guilty and worthy of condemnation? The sinner is the Gospel's reason for existence. If you are undeserving, ill-deserving, hell-deserving, you are the
sort of man for whom the Gospel is ordained and arranged and proclaimed. God justifies the ungodly.

I want to make this very plain. I hope that I have
done so already. But, still, plain as it is, it is only the
Lord who can make a man see it. At first it does
seem most amazing to an awakened man that salvation
should really be for him when he is lost and guilty. He
thinks that it must be for him when he is penitent, forgetting that his penitence is a part of his salvation.
"Oh," he says, "but I must be this and that," all of which
is true, for he shall be this and that as the result of salvation. But salvation comes to him before he has any
of the results of salvation. It comes to him, in fact,
while he deserves only this bare, beggarly, base, abom-

inable description: *ungodly*. That is all he is when God's Gospel comes to justify him.

May I, therefore, urge upon any who have no good thing about them—who fear that they have not even a good feeling or anything whatever that can recommend them to God—to firmly believe that our gracious God is able and willing to take them without anything to recommend them, and to forgive them spontaneously, not because *they* are good, but because *He* is good. Does He not make His sun to shine on the evil as well as on the good? Does He not give fruitful seasons and send the rain and the sunshine in their time upon the most ungodly nations? Yes, even Sodom had its sun, and Gomorrah had its dew. The great grace of God surpasses my conception and your conception, and I would have you think worthily of it. As high as the heavens are above the earth, so high are God's thoughts above our thoughts. He can abundantly pardon. Jesus Christ came into the world to save sinners; forgiveness is for the guilty.

Do not attempt to touch yourself up and make yourself something other than you really are, but come as you are to Him who justifies the ungodly. A great artist some time ago had painted a picture of a part of the city in which he lived, and he wanted, for historic purposes, to include in his picture certain characters well known in the town. A street sweeper who was unkempt, ragged, and filthy, was known to everybody, and there was a suitable place for him in the picture. The artist said to this ragged and rugged individual, "I will pay you well if you will come down to my studio and let me paint you." He came around in the morning, but he was soon sent away, for he had washed his face, combed his hair, and donned a respectable suit of clothes. He was needed as a beggar and was not invited in any other capacity. Even so, the Gospel will receive you into its halls if you come as a sinner, not otherwise. Wait not for reformation, but come at once for salvation. God justifieth *the ungodly*, and that takes *you* up where you now are; it meets you in your worst estate.

Come in your disorder. I mean, come to your heavenly Father in all your sin and sinfulness. Come to Jesus just as you are: leprous, filthy, naked, neither fit to live nor fit to die. Come, you that are the very sweepings of creation; come, though you hardly dare to hope for anything but death. Come, though despair is brooding over you, pressing upon your bosom like a horrible nightmare. Come and ask the Lord to justify another ungodly one. Why should He not? Come, for this great mercy of God is meant for such as you. I put it in the language of the text, and I cannot put it more strongly: the Lord God Himself takes to Himself this gracious title, "Him that justifieth the ungodly." He makes just, and causes to be treated as just, those who by nature are ungodly. Is not that a wonderful word for you? Do not delay till you have considered this matter well.

4

"It Is God That Justifieth"

IT IS A WONDERFUL THING to be justified or made just. If we had never broken the laws of God we would not have needed it, for we should have been just in ourselves. He who has all his life done the things which he should have done, and has never done anything which he should not have done, is justified by the Law. But you are not one of that sort, I am quite sure. You have too much honesty to pretend to be without sin, and therefore you need to be justified.

Now, if you justify yourself, you will simply be a self-deceiver. Therefore, do not attempt it. It is never worthwhile. If you ask your fellow mortals to justify you, what can they do? You can make some of them speak well of you for small favors, and others will backbite you for less. Their judgment is not worth much.

Our text says, "It is God that justifieth," and this is much more to the point. It is an astonishing fact, and one that we should consider with care. Come and see.

In the first place, nobody else but God would ever have thought of justifying those who are guilty. They have lived in open rebellion; they have done evil with both hands; they have gone from bad to worse; they have turned back to sin even after they have smarted

19

for it, and have therefore for a while been forced to
leave it. They have broken the Law and trampled on
the Gospel. They have refused proclamations of mercy
and have persisted in ungodliness. How can they be
forgiven and justified? Their fellowmen, despairing
of them, say, "They are hopeless cases." Even Christians look upon them with sorrow rather than with
hope. But not so their God. He, in the splendor of His
electing grace having chosen some of them before the
foundation of the world, will not rest till He has justified them and made them to be accepted in the beloved. Is it not written, "Whom he did predestinate,
them he also called: and whom he called, them he also
justified: and whom he justified, them he also glorified"
(Ro 8:30)? Thus you see there are some whom the
Lord resolves to justify. Why should not you and I be
of the number?

None but God would ever have thought of justifying
me. I am a wonder to myself. I doubt not that grace
is equally seen in others. Look at Saul of Tarsus who
foamed at the mouth against God's servants. Like a
hungry wolf, he worried the lambs and the sheep right
and left. And yet God struck him down on the road to
Damascus and changed his heart and so fully justified
him that before long this man became the greatest
preacher of justification by faith that ever lived. He
must often have marveled that he was justified by faith
in Christ Jesus, for he was once a determined stickler
for salvation by the works of the Law. None but God
would have ever thought of justifying such a man as
Saul the persecutor, but the Lord God is glorious in
grace.

But, even if anybody had thought of justifying the ungodly, none but God could have done it. It is quite impossible for any person to forgive offenses which have not been committed against himself. A person has greatly injured you. You can forgive him, and I hope you will, but no third person can forgive him apart from you. If the wrong is done to you, the pardon must come from you. If we have sinned against God, it is in God's power to forgive; for the sin is against Himself. That is why David says in Psalm 51: 4, "Against thee, thee only, have I sinned, and done this evil in thy sight," for then God, against whom the offense is committed, can put the offense away. That which we owe to God, our great Creator can remit if it so pleases Him; and if He remits it, it is remitted. None but the great God against whom we have committed the sin can blot out that sin; let us, therefore, see that we go to Him and seek mercy at His hands. Do not let us be led aside by those who would have us confess to them; they have no warrant in the Word of God for their pretensions. But even if they were ordained to pronounce absolution in God's name, it would still be better to go ourselves to the great Lord through Jesus Christ, the Mediator, and seek and find pardon at His hands, since we are sure that this is the right way. Proxy religion involves too great a risk; you had better see to your soul's matters yourself and leave them in no man's hands.

Only God can justify the ungodly, but He can do it to perfection. He casts our sins behind His back; He blots them out. He says that though they be sought for, they shall not be found. With no other reason for it but

His own infinite goodness, He has prepared a glorious
way by which He can make scarlet sins as white as
snow, and remove our transgressions from us as far as
the East is from the West. He says, "I will not remember your sins." He goes the length of making an end
of sin. One of old called out in amazement, "Who is a
God like unto thee, that pardoneth iniquity, and passeth by the transgression of the remnant of his heritage?
He retaineth not his anger for ever, because he delight-
eth in mercy" (Mic 7:18).

We are not now speaking of justice, nor of God's
dealing with men according to their deserts. If you
profess to deal with the righteous Lord on Law terms,
everlasting wrath threatens you, for that is what you
deserve. Blessed be His name, He has not dealt with
us after our sins; but now He treats with us on terms
of free grace and infinite compassion, and He says, "I
will receive you graciously and love you freely." Believe
it, for it is certainly true that the great God is able to
treat the guilty with abundant mercy; yes, He is able
to treat the ungodly as if they had been always godly.
Read carefully the parable of the prodigal son, and see
how the forgiving father received the returning wan-
derer with as much love as if he had never gone away
and had never defiled himself with harlots. So far did
he carry this that the elder brother began to grumble
at it, but the father never withdrew his love. However
guilty you may be, if you will only come back to your
God and Father, He will treat you as if you had never
done wrong! He will regard you as just, and deal with
you accordingly. What do you say to this?

Do you not see—for I want to bring out clearly what a splendid thing it is—that as none but God would think of justifying the ungodly, and none but God could do it, yet the Lord can do it? See how the apostle puts the challenge, "Who shall lay any thing to the charge of God's elect? It is God that justifieth" (Ro 8:33). If God has justified a man it is well done, it is rightly done, it is justly done, it is everlastingly done. I read a statement in a magazine which is full of venom against the Gospel and those who preach it, that we hold some kind of theory by which we imagine that sin can be removed from men. We hold no theory; we publish a fact. The grandest fact under heaven is this: Christ by His precious blood does actually put away sin; and God, for Christ's sake dealing with men on terms of divine mercy, forgives the guilty and justifies them, not according to anything that He sees in them or foresees will be in them, but according to the riches of His mercy which lie in His own heart. This we have preached, do preach, and will preach as long as we live. "It is God that justifieth" the ungodly; He is not ashamed of doing it, nor are we of preaching it.

The justification which comes from God Himself must be beyond question. If the Judge acquits me, who can condemn me? If the highest court in the universe has pronounced me just, who shall lay anything to my charge? Justification from God is a sufficient answer to an awakened conscience. The Holy Spirit by its means breathes peace over our entire nature, and we are no longer afraid. With this justification we can answer all the roarings and railings of Satan and ungodly men. With this we shall be able to die; with this we shall boldly rise again and face the last great court of justice.

> Bold shall I stand in that great day,
> For who aught to my charge shall lay?
> While by my Lord absolved I am
> From sin's tremendous curse and blame.

> ZINZENDORF

The Lord can blot out all your sins. I make no shot in the dark when I say this. "All manner of sin and blasphemy shall be forgiven unto men" (Mt 12:31). Though you are steeped up to your throat in crime, He can with a word remove the defilement and say, "I will, be thou clean." The Lord is a great Forgiver.

"I believe in the forgiveness of sins." Do *you?*

He can even at this hour pronounce the sentence, "Thy sins be forgiven thee; go in peace"; and if He does this, no power in heaven or earth or under the earth can put you under suspicion, much less under wrath. Do not doubt the power of almighty love. You could not forgive your fellowman had he offended you as you have offended God, but you must not measure God's corn with your bushel. His thoughts and ways are as much above yours as the heavens are high above the earth.

"Well," you say, "it would be a great miracle if the Lord were to pardon me." Indeed, it would be a supreme miracle; therefore, He is likely to do it, for He does "great things and unsearchable" (Job 5:9) which we looked not for.

I was myself stricken down with a horrible sense of

guilt which made my life a misery. But when I heard
the command, "Look unto me, and be ye saved, all the
ends of the earth, for I am God, and there is none else"
(Is 45:22), I looked, and in a moment the Lord justified me. Jesus Christ, made sin for me, was what I
saw, and that sight gave me rest. When those who
were bitten by the fiery serpents in the wilderness
looked to the serpent of brass, they were healed at once;
and so was I when I looked to the crucified Saviour.
The Holy Spirit, who enabled me to believe, gave me
peace through believing. I felt as sure that I was forgiven as I had felt sure of condemnation before. I had
been certain of my condemnation because the Word of
God declared it, and my conscience bore witness to it;
but when the Lord justified me I was made equally
certain by the same witnesses. The word of the Lord
in the Scripture says, "He that believeth on him is not
condemned" (Jn 3:18). My conscience bears witness
that I believed, and that God in pardoning me is just.
Thus I have the witness of the Holy Spirit and my own
conscience, and these two agree in one. Oh, how I wish
you would receive the testimony of God upon this matter, and then soon you would also have the witness in
yourself!

I venture to say that a sinner justified by God stands
on even a surer footing than a righteous man justified
by his works, if there be such. We could never be surer
that we had done enough works; conscience would always be uneasy for fear that, after all, we should come
short, and we could only have the trembling verdict of
a fallible judgment to rely upon. But when God Himself justifies and the Holy Spirit bears witness thereto

by giving us peace with God, then we feel that the matter is sure and settled and we enter into rest. No tongue can tell the depth of that calm which comes over the soul which has received the peace of God which passeth all understanding.

5

Just and the Justifier

WE HAVE SEEN the ungodly justified, and have considered the great truth that only God can justify any man. We now come a step further and make the inquiry, How can a just God justify guilty men? We find a full answer in the words of Paul in Romans 3:21-26. We will read six verses from the chapter in order to get the main idea of the passage:

> But now the righteousness of God without the law is manifested, being witnessed by the law and the prophets; even the righteousness of God which is by faith of Jesus Christ unto all and upon all them that believe: for there is no difference: for all have sinned, and come short of the glory of God: being justified freely by his grace through the redemption that is in Christ Jesus: whom God hath set forth to be a propitiation through faith in his blood, to declare his righteousness for the remission of sins that are past, through the forbearance of God; to declare, I say, at this time his righteousness; that he might be just, and the justifier of him which believeth in Jesus.

Let me give you a bit of personal experience. When I was under conviction of sin, under the hand of the

Holy Spirit, I had a clear and sharp sense of the justice
of God. Sin, whatever it might be to other people, became to me an intolerable burden. It was not so much
that I feared hell, but that I feared sin. I knew myself
to be so horribly guilty that I remember feeling that if
God did not punish me for sin He should do so. I felt
that the Judge of all the earth ought to condemn such
sin as mine. I sat on the judgment seat and condemned
myself to perish, for I confessed that had I been God
I could have done nothing else than send such a guilty
creature as I was down to the lowest hell.

All the while, I had on my mind a deep concern for
the honor of God's name and the integrity of His moral
government. I felt that it would not satisfy my conscience if I could be forgiven unjustly. The sin I had
committed must be punished. But then there was the
question of how God could be just and yet justify me
who had been so guilty. I asked my heart: "How can
He be just and yet the Justifier?" I was worried and
wearied with this question; I could see no answer to it.
Certainly, I could never have invented an answer
which would have satisfied my conscience.

The doctrine of the atonement is to my mind one of
the surest proofs of the divine inspiration of Holy
Scripture. Who would or could have thought of the
just Ruler dying for the unjust rebel? This is no teaching of human mythology or dream of poetical imagination. This method of expiation is only known among
men because it is a fact; fiction coulld not have devised
it. God Himself ordained it; it is not a matter which
could have been imagined.

I had heard the plan of salvation by the sacrifice of

Jesus from my youth, but I did not know any more about it in my innermost soul than if I had been born and bred a Hottentot. The light was there, but I was blind; it was of necessity that the Lord Himself should make it plain to me. It came to me as a new revelation, as fresh as if I had never read in Scripture that Jesus was declared to be the propitiation for sins that God might be just. I believe it will have to come as a revelation to every newborn child of God whenever he sees it; I mean that glorious doctrine of the substitution of the Lord Jesus. I came to understand that salvation was possible through vicarious sacrifice, and that provision had been made in the first constitution and arrangement of things for such a substitution.

I was made to see that He who is the Son of God, co-equal and co-eternal with the Father, had of old been made the covenant Head of a chosen people that He might in that capacity suffer for them and save them. Inasmuch as our Fall was not at first a personal one, for we fell in our federal representative, the first Adam, it became possible for us to be recovered by a second representative, even by Him who has undertaken to be the covenant Head of His people in order to be their second Adam. I saw that before I actually sinned I had fallen by my first father's sin, and I rejoiced that therefore it became possible in point of law for me to rise by a second Head and Representative. The Fall by Adam left a loophole of escape; another Adam can undo the ruin made by the first.

When I was anxious about the possibility of a just God pardoning me, I understood and saw by faith that He who is the Son of God became man and in His own

blessed person bore my sin in His own body on the
tree. I saw the chastisement of my peace was laid on
Him, and that with His stripes I was healed. Have you
ever seen that? Have you ever understood how God
can be just to the full, not remitting penalty nor blunt-
ing the edge of the sword, and yet can be infinitely merciful and can justify the ungodly who turn to Him?

It was because the Son of God, supremely glorious in
His matchless person, undertook to vindicate the Law
by bearing the sentence due to me that therefore God
is able to pass by my sin. The Law of God was more
vindicated by the death of Christ than it would have
been had all transgressors been sent to hell. For the
Son of God to suffer for sin was a more glorious estab-
lishment of the government of God than for the whole
race to suffer.

Jesus has borne the death penalty on our behalf.
Behold the wonder! There He hangs upon the cross!
This is the greatest sight you will ever see. Son of God
and Son of man, there He hangs, bearing pains unut-
terable, the Just for the unjust, to bring us to God. Oh
the glory of that sight! The Innocent punished! The
Holy One condemned! The ever-blessed One made a
curse! The infinitely glorious One put to a shameful
death! The more I look at the sufferings of the Son of
God, the more sure I am that they must meet my case.
Why did He suffer if not to turn aside the penalty from
us? If, then, He turned it aside by His death, it is
turned aside; and those who believe in Him need not
fear it. It must be so that since expiation is made, God
is able to forgive without shaking the basis of His
throne or in the least degree blotting the statute book.

Conscience gets a full answer to her tremendous question.

The wrath of God against iniquity, whatever that may be, must be terrible beyond all conception. Well did Moses say, "Who knoweth the power of thine anger?" (Ps 90:11). Yet, when we hear the Lord of glory cry, "Why hast thou forsaken me?" (Mt 27:46) and see Him yielding up the ghost, we feel that the justice of God has received abundant vindication by obedience so perfect and death so terrible, rendered by so divine a person. If God Himself bows before His own Law, what more can be done? There is more in the atonement by way of merit than there is in all human sin by way of demerit.

The great gulf of Jesus' loving self-sacrifice can swallow up the mountains of our sins, all of them. For the sake of the infinite good of this one representative Man, the Lord may well look with favor upon other men, however unworthy they may be in and of themselves. It was a miracle of miracles that the Lord Jesus Christ should stand in our stead and

> Bear that we might never bear
> His Father's righteous ire.

But He has done so. "It is finished" (Jn 19:30). God will spare the sinner because He did not spare His Son. God can pass by your transgressions because He laid those transgressions upon His only begotten Son nearly 2,000 years ago. If you believe in Jesus (that is the point), then your sins were carried away by Him who was the scapegoat for His people.

What is it to believe in Him? It is not merely to

say, "He is God and the Saviour," but to trust Him
wholly and entirely and take Him for all your salvation from this time forth and forever as your Lord,
your Master, your all. If you will have Jesus, He has
you already. If you believe on Him, I tell you that you
cannot go to hell, for that would make the sacrifice of
Christ of none effect. It cannot be that a sacrifice
would be accepted and yet the soul should die for
whom that sacrifice has been received. If the believing
soul could be condemned, then why a sacrifice? If
Jesus died in my stead, why should I die also?

Every believer can claim that the sacrifice was actually made for him. By faith he has laid his hands on
it and made it his own, and therefore he may rest assured that he can never perish. The Lord would not
receive this offering on our behalf and then condemn
us to die. The Lord cannot read our pardon written in
the blood of His own Son and then smite us. That
would be impossible. Oh that you may have grace
given you at once to look away to Jesus and to begin
at the beginning, with Jesus who is the fountainhead
of mercy to guilty man!

"He justifieth the ungodly." "It is God that justifieth," therefore, and for that reason only it can be
done; and He does it through the atoning sacrifice of
His divine Son. Therefore it can be justly done—so
justly done that none will ever question it—so thoroughly done that in the last tremendous day, when heaven
and earth shall pass away, there shall be none that
shall deny the validity of the justification. "Who is he
that condemneth? It is Christ that died. Who shall

lay any thing to the charge of God's elect? It is God
that justifieth" (Ro 8:34, 33).

Now will you come into this lifeboat just as you are?
Here is safety from the wreck! Accept the sure deliverance. "I have nothing with me," you say. You are not
asked to bring anything with you. Men who escape
for their lives will leave even their clothes behind.
Leap for it, just as you are.

I will tell you something about myself to encourage
you. My sole hope for heaven lies in the full atonement made upon Calvary's cross for the ungodly. On
that I firmly rely. I have not the shadow of a hope
anywhere else. You are in the same condition as I
am, for neither of us has anything of our own worth
as a ground of trust. Let us join hands and stand
together at the foot of the cross and trust our souls
once for all to Him who shed His blood for the guilty.
We will be saved by one and the same Saviour. If you
perish trusting Him, I must perish too. What can I do
more to prove my own confidence in the Gospel which
I set before you?

6

Deliverance from Sinning

I WOULD LIKE TO SAY a plain word or two to those who understand the method of justification by faith which is in Christ Jesus, but whose trouble is that they cannot cease from sin. We can never be happy, restful, or spiritually healthy till we become holy. We must get rid of sin, but how can we? This is the life-or-death question of many. The old nature is very strong, and they have tried to curb and tame it. But it will not be subdued, and they find themselves, though anxious to be better, if anything, growing worse than before.

The heart is so hard, the will is so obstinate, the passions are so furious, the thoughts are so volatile, the imagination is so ungovernable, the desires are so wild, that the man feels that he has a den of wild beasts within him which will eat him up sooner than they will be ruled by him. We may say of our fallen nature what the Lord said to Job concerning Leviathan: "Wilt thou play with him as with a bird? Or wilt thou bind him for thy maidens?" (41:5). A man might as well hope to hold the north wind in the hollow of his hand as expect to control by his own strength those boisterous powers which dwell within his fallen nature. This is a greater feat than any of the fabled labors of Hercules; God is wanted here.

"I could believe that Jésus would forgive sin," says one, "but then my trouble is that I sin again, and that I feel such awful tendencies to evil within me. As surely as a stone, if it be flung up into the air, soon comes down again to the ground, so do I, though I am sent up to heaven by earnest preaching, return again to my insensible state. Alas! I am easily fascinated with the spell-binding eyes of sin, and am thus held as under a spell, that I cannot escape from my own folly."

Salvation would be a sadly incomplete affair if it did not deal with this part of our ruined estate. We want to be purified as well as pardoned. Justification without sanctification would not be salvation at all. It would call the leper clean and leave him to die of his disease; it would forgive the rebellion and allow the rebel to remain an enemy to his king. It would remove the consequences but overlook the cause, and this would leave an endless and hopeless task before us. It would stop the stream for a time but leave an open fountain of defilement which would sooner or later break forth with increased power. Remember that the Lord Jesus came to take away sin in three ways. He came to remove the penalty of sin, the power of sin, and last, the presence of sin. At once you may reach the second part, the power of sin may immediately be broken, and so you will be on the road to the third, namely, the removal of the presence of sin. We "know that he was manifested to take away our sins" (1 Jn 3:5).

The angel said of our Lord, "Thou shalt call his

name JESUS: for he shall save his people from their sins" (Mt 1:21). Our Lord Jesus came to destroy in us the works of the devil. That which was said at our Lord's birth was also declared in His death; for when the soldier pierced His side, there came out blood and water to set forth the double cure by which we are delivered from the guilt and the defilement of sin.

If, however, you are troubled about the power of sin and about the tendencies of your nature, as you well may be, here is a promise for you. Have faith in it, for it stands in that covenant of grace which is ordered in all things and sure. God, who cannot lie, has said in Ezekiel 36:26, "A new heart also will I give you, and a new spirit will I put within you: and I will take away the stony heart out of your flesh, and I will give you an heart of flesh."

You see, it is all "I will" and "I will." "I will give" and "I will take away." This is the royal style of the King of kings who is able to accomplish all His will. No word of His shall ever fall to the ground.

The Lord knows very well that you cannot change your own heart and cannot cleanse your own nature, but He also knows that He can do both. He can cause the Ethiopian to change his skin, and the leopard his spots. Hear this and be astonished: He can create you a second time; He can cause you to be born again. This is a miracle of grace, but the Holy Spirit will perform it. It would be a very wonderful thing if one could stand at the foot of the Niagara Falls and could speak a word which would make the Niagara River begin to run upstream and leap up that great precipice over which it now rolls down in stupendous force. Nothing but the power of God could achieve that marvel, but that would be more than a fit parallel to what would take place if the course of your nature were altogether reversed. All things are possible with God. He can reverse the direction of your desires and the current of your life; and instead of going downward from God, He can make your whole being tend upward toward God. In fact, that is what the Lord has promised to do for all who are in the covenant, and we know from Scripture that all believers are in the covenant. Let me read the words again: "A new spirit will I put within you: and I will take away the stony heart out of your flesh, and I will give you an heart of flesh" (Eze 36:26).

What a wonderful promise! And it is yea and amen in Christ Jesus to the glory of God by us. Let us lay hold of it, accept it as true, and appropriate it to ourselves. Then shall it be fulfilled in us, and we shall have, in after days and years, to sing of that wondrous change which the sovereign grace of God has made in us.

It is worthy of consideration that when the Lord takes away the stony heart, that deed is done; and when that is once done, no known power can ever take away that new heart which He gives and that right spirit which He puts within us. "The gifts and calling of God are without repentance" (Ro 11:29), that is, without repentance on His part; He does not take away what He once has given. Let Him renew you and you will be renewed. Man's reformations and cleanings up soon come to an end, for the dog returns to his vomit. But when God puts a new heart in us, the new heart

is there forever and it never will harden into stone
again. He who made it flesh will keep it so. Herein we
may rejoice and be glad forever in that which God
creates in the kingdom of His grace.

To put the matter very simply, did you ever hear of
Rowland Hill's illustration of the cat and the sow? I
will give it in my own fashion, to illustrate our Saviour's
expressive words, "Ye must be born again" (Jn 3:7).
Do you see that cat? What a clean creature she is!
How cleverly she washes herself with her tongue and
her paws! It is quite a pretty sight! Did you ever see
a sow do that? No, you never did. It is contrary to
its nature. It prefers to wallow in the mire. Go and
teach a sow to wash itself, and see how little success
you would gain. It would be a great sanitary improve-
ment if swine would be clean. Teach them to wash and
clean themselves as the cat has been doing! It is a useless task. You may by force wash that sow, but it has-
tens to the mire and is soon as foul as ever. The only
way in which you can get a sow to wash itself is to
transform it into a cat; then it will wash and be clean,
but not till then!

Suppose that transformation had been accomplished,
and then what was difficult or impossible is easy
enough; the swine will henceforth be fit for your parlor
and your hearth rug. So it is with an ungodly man;
you cannot force him to do what a renewed man does
most willingly. You may teach him and set him a good
example, but he cannot learn the art of holiness because he does not want to; his nature leads him another
way. When the Lord makes a new man of him, then
all things wear a different aspect. So great is this

change that I once heard a convert say, "Either all the world is changed, or else I am." The new nature follows after right as naturally as the old nature wanders after wrong. What a blessing to receive such a nature! Only the Holy Spirit can give it.

Did it ever strike you what a wonderful thing it is for the Lord to give a new heart and a right spirit to a man? Perhaps you have seen a lobster which has fought with another lobster and lost one of its claws, and a new claw has grown. That is a remarkable thing, but it is a much more astounding fact that a man should have a new heart given to him. This, indeed, is a miracle beyond the powers of nature. There is a tree. If you cut off one of its limbs, another one may grow in its place. But can you change the tree? Can you sweeten sour sap? Can you make the thorn bear figs? You can graft something better into it, and that is the analogy which nature gives us of the work of grace; but to absolutely change the vital sap of the tree would be a miracle indeed. Such a prodigy and mystery of power God works in all who believe in Jesus.

If you yield yourself up to His divine working, the Lord will alter your nature; He will subdue the old nature and breathe new life into you. Put your trust in the Lord Jesus Christ, and He will take the stony heart out of your flesh and will give you a heart of flesh. Where everything was hard, everything shall be tender; where everything was vicious, everything shall be virtuous; where everything tended downward, everything shall rise upward with impetuous force. The lion of anger shall give place to the lamb of meek-

ness; the raven of uncleanness shall fly before the dove
of purity; the vile serpent of deceit shall be trodden
under the heel of truth.

I have seen with my own eyes such marvelous
changes of moral and spiritual character that I despair
of none. I could, if it were fitting, point out those who
were once unchaste women who are now pure as the
driven snow, and blaspheming men who now delight
everyone around them by their intense devotion.
Thieves are made honest, drunkards sober, liars truthful, and scoffers zealous. Wherever the grace of God
has appeared to a man it has trained him to deny "ungodliness and worldly lusts," and to "live soberly, right-
eously, and godly, in this present world" (Titus 2:12),
and it will do the same for you.

"I cannot make this change," says someone. Who
said you could? The Scripture which we have quoted
speaks not of what man will do, but of what God will
do. It is God's promise, and it is for Him to fulfill His
own engagements. Trust in Him to fulfill His Word to
you, and it will be done.

"But how is it to be done?" What business is that
of yours? Must the Lord explain His methods before
you will believe Him? The Lord's working in this matter is a great mystery; the Holy Spirit performs it. He
who made the promise has the responsibility of keeping the promise, and He is equal to the occasion. God,
who promises this marvelous change, will assuredly
carry it out in all who receive Jesus, for to all of them
He gives power to become the sons of God.

Oh that you would believe it! Oh that you would do
the gracious Lord the justice to believe that He can and

will do this for you, great miracle though it will be! Oh that you would believe that God cannot lie! Oh that you would trust Him for a new heart and a right spirit, for He can give them to you! May the Lord give you faith in His promise, faith in His Son, faith in the Holy Spirit, and faith in Him, and to Him shall be praise and honor and glory forever and ever! Amen.

7

By Grace Through Faith

I THINK IT WELL to turn a little to one side that I may ask you to observe adoringly the fountainhead of our salvation, which is the grace of God. "By grace are ye saved" (Eph 2:8). Because God is gracious, therefore sinful men are forgiven, converted, purified, and saved. It is not because of anything in them or that ever can be in them that they are saved, but because of the boundless love, goodness, pity, compassion, mercy, and grace of God. Tarry a moment, then, at the wellhead. Behold the pure river of water of life as it proceeds out of the throne of God and of the Lamb!

What an abyss is the grace of God! Who can measure its breadth? Who can fathom its depth? Like all the rest of the divine attributes, it is infinite. God is full of love, for "God is love." God is full of goodness; the very name "God" is short for "good." Unbounded goodness and love enter into the very essence of the Godhead. It is because "his mercy endureth for ever" (Ps 107:1) that men are not destroyed; because "his compassions fail not" (Lam 3:22), sinners are brought to Him and forgiven.

Remember this or you may fall into error by fixing

your minds so much upon the faith which is the channel of salvation that you will forget the grace which is the fountain and source even of faith itself. Faith is the work of God's grace in us. "No man can say that Jesus is the Lord, but by the Holy Ghost" (1 Co 12:3). "No man can come unto me," said Jesus, "except the Father which hath sent me draw him" (Jn 6:44). So that faith, which is coming to Christ, is the result of divine drawing. Grace is the first and last moving cause of salvation, and faith, essential as it is, is only an important part of the machinery which grace employs. We are saved "through faith," but salvation is "by grace." Sound forth those words as with the archangel's trumpet: "By grace are ye saved." What glad tidings for the undeserving!

Faith occupies the position of a channel or conduit pipe. Grace is the fountain and the stream; faith is the aqueduct along which the flood of mercy flows down to refresh the thirsty sons of men. It is a great pity when the aqueduct is broken. It is a sad sight to see around Rome the many noble aqueducts which no longer convey water into the city, because the arches are broken and the marvelous structures are in ruins. The aqueduct must be kept entire to convey the current. Similarly, faith must be true and sound, leading right up to God and coming right down to ourselves, that it may become a serviceable channel of mercy to our souls.

Still, I again remind you that faith is only the channel or aqueduct, and not the fountainhead, and we must not look so much to it that we exalt it above the divine source of all blessing which lies in the grace of

God. Never make a Christ out of your faith, nor think of as if it were the independent source of your salvation. Our life is found in "looking unto Jesus" (Heb 12:2), not in looking to our own faith. By faith all things become possible to us, yet the power is not in the faith but in the God upon whom faith relies. Grace is the powerful engine, and faith is the chain by which the carriage of the soul is attached to the great motive power. The righteousness of faith is not the moral excellence of faith but the righteousness of Jesus Christ which faith grasps and appropriates. The peace within the soul is not derived from the contemplation of our own faith, but it comes to us from Him who is our peace, the hem of whose garment faith touches, and virtue comes out of Him into the soul.

See, then, that the weakness of your faith will not destroy you. A trembling hand may receive a golden gift. The Lord's salvation can come to us though we have only faith as a grain of mustard seed. The power lies in the grace of God and not in our faith. Great messages can be sent along slender wires, and the peace-giving witness of the Holy Spirit can reach the heart by means of a threadlike faith which seems almost unable to sustain its own weight. Think more of Him to whom you look than of the look itself. You must look away even from your own looking and see nothing but Jesus and the grace of God revealed in Him.

8

What Is Faith?

WHAT IS THIS FAITH concerning which it is said, "By grace are ye saved, *through faith*"? There are many descriptions of faith, but almost all the definitions I have heard have made me understand it less than I did before I saw them. Someone said when he read the chapter that he would *confound* it, and it is very likely that he did so, though he meant to *expound* it. We may explain faith till nobody understands it. I hope I shall not be guilty of that fault. Faith is the simplest of all things, and perhaps because of its simplicity it is the more difficult to explain.

What is faith? It is made up of three things—knowledge, belief, and trust. Knowledge comes first. "How shall they believe in him of whom they have not heard?" (Ro 10:14). I want to be informed of a fact before I can possibly believe it. "Faith cometh by hearing" (Ro 10:17); we must first hear in order that we may know what is to be believed. "They that know thy name will put their trust in thee" (Ps 9:10). A measure of knowledge is essential to faith, hence the importance of getting knowledge. "Incline your ear, and come unto me: hear, and your soul shall live" (Is

55:3). Such was the word of the ancient prophet, and
it is the word of the Gospel still. Search the Scriptures
and learn what the Holy Spirit teaches concerning
Christ and His salvation. Seek to know God, "for he
that cometh to God must believe that he is, and that
he is a rewarder of them that diligently seek him" (Heb
11:6). May the Holy Spirit give you the spirit of
knowledge, and of the fear of the Lord! Know the
Gospel; know what the Good News is, how it talks of
free forgiveness and of change of heart, of adoption
into the family of God, and of countless other blessings. Know especially Christ Jesus the Son of God,
the Saviour of men, united to us by His human nature,
and yet one with God. And thus He was able to act as
Mediator between God and man, able to lay His hand
upon both and to be the connecting link between the
sinner and the Judge of all the earth. Endeavor to
know more and more of Christ Jesus. Endeavor especially to know the doctrine of the sacrifice of Christ,
for the point upon which saving faith mainly fixes itself is this: "God was in Christ, reconciling the world
unto himself, not imputing their trespasses unto them"
(2 Co 5:19). Know that Jesus was "made a curse for
us: for it is written, Cursed is every one that hangeth
on a tree (Gal 3:13). Drink deep of the doctrine of
the substitutionary work of Christ, for therein lies the
sweetest possible comfort to the guilty sons of men,
since the Lord "made him to be sin for us . . . that we
might be made the righteousness of God in him" (2 Co
5:21). Faith begins with knowledge.

The mind goes on to *believe* that these things are
true. The soul believes that God is and that He hears

the cries of sincere hearts, that the Gospel is from God, that justification by faith is the grand truth which God hath revealed in these last days by His Spirit more clearly than before. Then the heart believes that Jesus is verily and in truth our God and Saviour, the Redeemer of men, the Prophet, Priest, and King of His people. All this is accepted as sure truth, not to be questioned. I pray that you may at once come to this. Firmly believe that "the blood of Jesus Christ his [God's] Son cleanseth us from all sin" (1 Jn 1:7), that His sacrifice is complete and fully accepted of God on man's behalf, so that he that believeth on Jesus is not condemned. Believe these truths as you believe any other statements, for the difference between ordinary faith and saving faith lies mainly in the subjects in which it is placed. Believe the witness of God just as you believe the testimony of your own father or friend. "If we receive the witness of men, the witness of God is greater" (1 Jn 5:9).

So far you have made an advance toward faith; only one more ingredient is needed to complete it—trust. Commit yourself to the merciful God; rest your hope on the gracious Gospel. Trust your soul on the dying and living Saviour, wash away your sins in the atoning blood, accept His perfect righteousness, and all will be well. Trust is the lifeblood of faith; there is no saving faith without it. The Puritans were accustomed to explain faith by the word "recumbency." It meant leaning upon a thing. Lean with all your weight upon Christ. It would be a better illustration still if I said, fall at full length and lie on the rock of ages. Cast yourself upon Jesus. Rest in Him. Commit yourself to

Him. That done, you have exercised saving faith. Faith is not a blind thing, for faith begins with knowledge. It is not a speculative thing, for faith believes facts of which it is sure. It is not an unpractical, dreamy thing, for faith trusts and stakes its destiny upon the truth of revelation. That is one way of describing what faith is.

Let me try again. Faith is believing that Christ is what He is said to be and that He will do what He has promised to do, and then to expect this of Him. The Scriptures speak of Jesus Christ as being God in human flesh, as being perfect in His character, as being made a sin offering on our behalf, as bearing our sins in His own body on the tree. The Scripture speaks of Him as having finished transgression, made an end of sin, and brought in everlasting righteousness. The sacred records further tell us that He "rose again" (1 Co 15:4) from the dead, that He "ever liveth to make intercession for us" (Heb 7:25), that He has gone up into glory and has taken possession of heaven on the behalf of His people, and that He will shortly come again "to judge the . . . world with righteousness, and the peoples with equity" (Ps 98:9, ASV). We are most firmly to believe that it is so, for this is the testimony of God the Father when He said, "This is my beloved Son; hear him" (Lk 9:35). This also is testified by God the Holy Spirit, for the Spirit has borne witness to Christ, both in the inspired Word and by divers miracles and by His working in the hearts of men. We are to believe this testimony to be true.

Faith also believes that Christ will do what He has promised; that since He has promised to cast out none that come to Him, it is certain that He will not cast *us* out if we come to Him. Faith believes that since Jesus said, "The water that I shall give him shall be in him a well of water springing up into everlasting life" (Jn 4:14), it must be true; and if we get this living water from Christ, it will abide in us and will well up within us in streams of holy life. Whatever Christ has promised to do He will do, and we must believe this in order to look for pardon, justification, preservation, and eternal glory from His hands, according as He has promised them to believers in Him.

Then comes the next necessary step. Jesus is what He is said to be. Jesus will do what He says He will do. Therefore, we must each trust Him, saying, "He will be to me what He says He is, and He will do to me what He has promised to do. I leave myself in the hands of Him who is appointed to save, that He may save me. I rest upon His promise that He will do even as He has said." This is saving faith, and he that has it has everlasting life. Whatever his dangers and difficulties, whatever his darkness and depression, whatever his infirmities and sins, he that believes thus on Christ Jesus is not condemned, and shall never come into condemnation.

May that explanation be of some service! I trust it may be used by the Spirit of God to direct you into immediate peace. "Be not afraid; only believe." Trust, and be at rest.

My fear is lest you should rest content with understanding what is to be done, and yet never do it. Better the poorest real faith actually at work than the best ideal of it left in the region of speculation. The great matter is to believe on the Lord Jesus at once. Never mind distinctions and definitions. A hungry man eats though he does not understand the composition of his food, the anatomy of his mouth, or the process of digestion; he lives because he eats. Another far more clever person understands thoroughly the science of nutrition, but if he does not eat he will die with all his knowledge. There are, no doubt, many at this hour in hell who understood the doctrine of faith but did not believe. On the other hand, not one who has trusted in the Lord Jesus has ever been cast out, though he may never have been able intelligently to define his faith. Oh, receive the Lord Jesus into your soul, and you shall live forever! "He that believeth on the Son hath everlasting life" (Jn 3:36).

9

How May Faith Be Illustrated?

To MAKE THE MATTER of faith clearer still, I will give you a few illustrations. Though the Holy Spirit alone can make you see, it is my duty and my joy to furnish all the light I can and to pray the divine Lord to open blind eyes. Oh that you would pray the same prayer for yourself!

The faith which saves has its analogies in the human frame.

It is the *eye* which looks. By the eye we bring into the mind that which is far away; we can bring the sun and the far-off stars into the mind by a glance of the eye. So by trust we bring the Lord Jesus near to us; and though He is far away in heaven, He enters into our heart. Only look to Jesus, for the hymn is strictly true:

> There is life in a look at the Crucified One,
> There is life at this moment for thee.

Faith is the hand which grasps. When our hand takes hold of anything for itself, it does precisely what faith does when it appropriates Christ and the blessings of His redemption. Faith says, "Jesus is mine." Faith hears of the pardoning blood and cries, "I accept it to pardon *me*." Faith calls the legacies of the dying Jesus her own. And they are her own, for faith is Christ's heir; He has given Himself and all that He has to faith. Take that which grace has provided for you. You will not be a thief, for you have a divine permit: "Whosoever will, let him take the water of life freely" (Rev 22:17). He who may have a treasure simply by grasping it will be foolish indeed if he remains poor.

Faith is the mouth which feeds upon Christ. Before food can nourish us, it must be received into us. This eating and drinking is a simple matter. We willingly receive into the mouth that which is our food, and then we consent that it should pass down into our inward parts, wherein it is taken up and absorbed into our bodily frame. Paul says in Romans 10:8, "The word is nigh thee, even in thy mouth." Now all that is to be done is to swallow it, to allow it to go down into the soul. Oh that men had an appetite! For he who is hungry and sees meat before him does not need to be taught how to eat. "Give me," said one, "a knife and a fork and a chance." He was fully prepared to do the rest. A heart which truly hungers and thirsts after Christ has but to know that He is freely given, and at once it will receive Him. If you are in such a case, do not hesitate to receive Jesus. You may be sure that you will never be blamed for doing so, for unto "as many as received him, to them gave he power to become the sons of God" (Jn 1:12). He never repulses one, but He authorizes all who come to remain sons forever.

The pursuits of life illustrate faith in many ways.

The farmer buries good seed in the earth and expects it not only to live but to be multiplied. He has faith in the covenant arrangement that "seed-time and harvest shall not cease," and he is rewarded for his faith.

The merchant places his money in the care of a banker and trusts completely the honesty and soundness of the bank. He entrusts his capital to another's hands and feels far more at ease than if he had the solid gold locked up in an iron safe.

The sailor trusts himself to the sea. When he swims he takes his foot from the bottom and rests upon the buoyant ocean. He could not swim if he did not wholly cast himself upon the water.

The goldsmith puts precious metal into the fire which seems eager to consume it, but he receives it back again from the furnace purified by the heat.

You cannot turn anywhere in life without seeing faith in operation between man and man or between man and natural law. Now, just as we trust in daily life, even so are we to trust in God as He is revealed in Christ Jesus.

Faith exists in different persons in various degrees, according to the amount of their knowledge or growth in grace. Sometimes faith is little more than a simple *clinging* to Christ, a sense of dependence and a willingness to depend. When you are down at the seaside you will see limpets sticking to the rock. You walk with a soft tread up to the rock, strike the mollusk a quick blow with a stick, and off he comes. Try the next limpet in that way. You have given him warning; he heard the blow with which you struck his neighbor, and he clings with all his might. You will never get him off! Strike, and strike again, but you might as well break the rock. The limpet does not know much, but he clings. He is not acquainted with the geological formation of the rock, but he clings. He can cling, and he has found something to cling to; this is all his stock of knowledge, and he uses it for his security and salvation. It is the limpet's life to cling to the rock, and it is the sinner's life to cling to Jesus. Thousands of God's people have no more faith than this; they know enough to cling to Jesus with all their heart and soul, and this suffices for present peace and eternal safety. Jesus Christ is to them a Saviour strong and mighty, a rock immovable and immutable; they cling to Him for dear life, and this clinging saves them. Cannot you cling? Do so at once.

Faith is seen when one man relies upon another because of a knowledge of the superiority of the other. This is a higher faith, the faith which knows the reason for its dependence and acts upon it. I do not think the limpet knows much about the rock, but as faith grows it becomes more and more intelligent. A blind man trusts himself with his guide because he knows that his friend can see, and, trusting, he walks where his guide conducts him. If the poor man is born blind he does not know what sight is, but he knows that there is such a thing as sight and that it is possessed by his friend. Therefore, he freely puts his hand into the hand of the seeing one and follows his leadership. "We walk by faith, not by sight" (2 Co 5:7). "Blessed are they that have not seen, and yet have believed" (Jn 20:29). This is an excellent image of faith. We know that Jesus has merit and power and blessing which we do not possess, and therefore we gladly trust ourselves to Him to be to us what we cannot be to ourselves. We trust Him as the blind man trusts his guide. He never betrays our confidence, but He "of God is made unto us wisdom, and righteousness, and sanctification, and redemption" (1 Co 1:30).

Every boy who goes to school has to exert faith while learning. His teacher teaches him geography and instructs him as to the form of the earth and the existence of certain great cities and empires. The boy does not himself know that these things are true, except that he believes his teacher and the books put into his hands. That is what you will have to do with Christ if you are to be saved; you must simply know because He tells you, believe because He assures you it is so, and trust yourself with Him because He promises you that salvation will be the result.

Almost all that you and I know has come to us by faith. A scientific discovery has been made, and we are sure of it. On what grounds do we believe it? On the authority of certain well-known men of learning whose reputations are established. We have never made or seen their experiments, but we believe their witness. You must do the same with regard to Jesus: because He teaches you certain truths you are to be His disciples, and believe His words; because He has performed certain acts you are to be His client, and trust yourself with Him. He is infinitely superior to you, and presents Himself to your confidence as your Master and Lord. If you will receive Him and His words you shall be saved.

Another and a higher form of faith is that faith

which grows out of love. Why does a boy trust his
father? The reason why the child trusts his father
is because he loves him. Blessed and happy are they
who have a sweet faith in Jesus, intertwined with deep
affection for Him, for this is a restful confidence. These
lovers of Jesus are charmed with His character and
delighted with His mission; they are carried away by
the loving-kindness that He has manifested, and therefore they cannot help trusting Him because they so
much admire, revere, and love Him.

The way of loving trust in the Saviour is illustrated
by a lady who is the wife of the most eminent physician
of the day. She is seized with a dangerous illness and
is smitten down by its power, yet she is wonderfully
calm and quiet because her husband has made this
disease his special study and has healed thousands who
were similarly afflicted. She is not in the least troubled,
for she feels perfectly safe in the hands of one so dear
to her and in whom skill and love are blended in their
highest forms. Her faith is reasonable and natural; her
husband, from every point of view, deserves it of her.

This is the kind of faith which the happiest of believers exercise toward Christ. There is no physician
like Him; none can save as He can. We love Him and
He loves us, and therefore we put ourselves into His
hands, accept whatever He prescribes, and do whatever
He bids. We feel that nothing can be wrongly ordered
while He is the Director of our affairs, for He loves us
too well to let us perish or suffer a single needless pang.

Faith is the root of obedience, and this may be
clearly seen in the affairs of life. When a captain
trusts a pilot to steer his vessel into port, he manages

the vessel according to his direction. When a traveler trusts a guide to conduct him over a difficult pass, he follows the track which his guide points out. When a patient believes in a physician, he carefully follows his prescriptions and directions. Faith which refuses to obey the commands of the Saviour is a mere pretence and will never save the soul. We trust Jesus to save us. He gives us directions as to the way of salvation; we follow those directions and are saved. Do not forget this. Trust Jesus and prove your trust by doing whatever He bids you.

A notable form of faith arises out of assured knowledge. This comes of growth in grace and is the faith which believes Christ because it knows Him and trusts Him because it has proved Him to be infallibly faithful. An old Christian was in the habit of writing T and P in the margin of her Bible whenever she had tried and proved a promise. How easy it is to trust a tried and proved Saviour! You cannot do this as yet, but you will do so. Everything must have a beginning. You will rise to strong faith in due time. This matured faith asks not for signs and tokens, but bravely believes. Look at the faith of the master mariner; I have often wondered at it. He looses his cable and steams away from the land. For days, weeks, or even months, he never sees sail or shore; yet on he goes day and night without fear, till one morning he finds himself exactly opposite to the desired haven toward which he has been steering. How has he found his way over the trackless deep? He has trusted in his compass, his nautical almanac, his glass, and the heavenly bodies; and obeying their guidance, without sighting land, he has steered so accurately that he has not to change a point to enter into port. It is a wonderful thing to sail or steam without sight. Spiritually it is a blessed thing to leave altogether the shores of sight and feeling and to say good-bye to inward feelings, cheering providences, signs, tokens, and so forth. It is glorious to be far out on the ocean of divine love, believing in God and steering for heaven straight by the direction of the Word of God. "Blessed are they that have not seen, and yet have believed"; to them shall be administered an abundant entrance at the last, and a safe voyage on the way. Will you put your trust in God in Christ Jesus? There I rest with joyous confidence. Come with me and believe our Father and our Saviour. Come at once.

10

Why Are We Saved by Faith?

WHY IS FAITH SELECTED as the channel of salvation?
No doubt this inquiry is often made. "By grace are ye
saved *through faith*" (Eph 2:8) is assuredly the doctrine of Holy Scripture and the ordinance of God, but
why is it so? Why is faith selected rather than hope
or love or patience?

It becomes us to be modest in answering such a
question, for God's ways are not always to be understood; nor are we allowed presumptuously to question
them. Humbly we would reply that, as far as we can
tell, faith has been selected as the channel of grace
because there is a natural adaptation in faith to be
used as the receiver. Suppose that I am about to give
a poor man some money. I put it into his hand. Why?
Well, it would hardly be fitting to put it into his ear
or to lay it upon his foot; the hand seems made on
purpose to receive. So, in our mental frame, faith is
created on purpose to be a receiver; it is the hand of
the man, and there is a fitness in receiving grace by its
means.

Do let me put this very plainly. Faith which receives
Christ is as simple an act as when your child receives

an apple from you, because you hold it out and promise to give him the apple if he comes for it. The belief
and the receiving relate only to an apple, but they
make up precisely the same act as the faith which deals
with eternal salvation. What the child's hand is to the
apple, that your faith is to the perfect salvation of
Christ. The child's hand does not make the apple nor
improve the apple nor deserve the apple; it only takes
it. And faith is chosen by God to be the receiver of
salvation, because it does not pretend to create salvation nor to help in it, but it is content to receive it humbly. "Faith is the tongue that begs pardon, the hand
which receives it, and the eye which sees it; but it is
not the price which buys it." Faith never makes herself her own plea; she rests all her argument upon the
blood of Christ. She becomes a good servant to bring
the riches of the Lord Jesus to the soul, because she
acknowledges whence she drew them and admits that
grace alone entrusted her with them.

Faith, again, is doubtless selected because it gives
all the glory to God. It is of faith that it might be
by grace, and it is of grace that there might be no
boasting, for God cannot endure pride. "The proud
he knoweth afar off" (Ps 138:6), and He has no wish
to come nearer to them. He will not give salvation in
a way which will suggest or foster pride. Paul says,
"Not of works, lest any man should boast" (Eph 2:9).
Now, faith excludes all boasting. The hand which receives charity does not say, "I am to be thanked for
accepting the gift"; that would be absurd. When the
hand conveys bread to the mouth it does not say to the
body, "Thank me, for I feed you." It is a very simple

thing that the hand does, though a very necessary thing, and it never arrogates glory to itself for what it does. So God has selected faith to receive the unspeakable gift of His grace, because it cannot take any credit to itself but must adore the gracious God who is the Giver of all good. Faith sets the crown upon the right head, and therefore the Lord Jesus was accustomed to putting the crown upon the head of faith, saying, "Thy faith hath saved thee; go in peace" (Lk 7:50).

Next, God selects faith as the channel of salvation because it is a sure method, linking man with God. When man confides in God, there is a point of union between them, and that union guarantees blessing. Faith saves us because it makes us cling to God and therefore brings us into connection with Him. I have often used the following illustration. Years ago a boat was upset above Niagara Falls. Two men were being carried down the current when persons on the shore managed to float a rope out to them. Both seized it. One of them held onto it and was safely drawn to the bank. But the other, seeing a great log come floating by, unwisely let go the rope and clung to the log, for it was bigger and apparently better to cling to. The log with the man on it went right over the vast abyss, because there was no union between the log and the shore. The size of the log was of no benefit to him who grasped it; it needed a connection with the shore to produce safety. So when a man trusts to his works or to sacraments or to anything of that sort, he will not be saved, because there is no junction between him and Christ. But faith, though it may seem to be like a slender cord, is in the hands of the great God on the shore side; infinite power pulls in the connecting line and thus draws the man from destruction. Oh, the blessedness of faith because it unites us to God!

Faith is chosen again because it touches the springs of action. Even in common things faith of a certain sort lies at the root of all. I wonder whether I am wrong if I say that we never do anything except through faith of some sort. If I walk across my study it is because I believe my legs will carry me. A man eats because he believes in the necessity of food; he goes to his business because he believes in the value of money; he accepts a check because he believes that the bank will honor it. Columbus discovered America because he believed that there was another continent beyond the ocean, and the Pilgrim fathers colonized it because they believed that God would be with them on those rocky shores. Most grand deeds have been born of faith; for good or for evil, faith works wonders by the man in whom it dwells.

Faith in its natural form is an all-prevailing force which enters into all manner of human actions. Possibly he who derides faith in God is the man who in an evil form has the most faith; indeed, he usually falls into a credulity which would be ridiculous if it were not disgraceful. God gives salvation to faith, because by creating faith in us He thus touches the real mainspring of our emotions and actions. He has, so to speak, taken possession of the battery and now He can send the sacred current to every part of our nature. When we believe in Christ, and the heart has come into the possession of God, then we are saved from sin and are moved toward repentance, holiness, zeal, prayer, consecration, and every other gracious thing. "What oil is to the wheels, what weights are to a clock, what wings are to a bird, what sails are to a ship, that faith is to all holy duties and services." Have faith, and all other graces will follow and continue to hold their course.

Faith, again, has the power of working by love; it influences the affections toward God and draws the heart after the best things. He who believes in God will beyond all question love God. Faith is an act of the understanding, but it also proceeds from the heart. "With the heart man believeth unto righteousness" (Ro 10:10). Hence, God gives salvation to faith because it resides next door to the affections and is closely related to love, and love is the parent and the nurse of every holy feeling and act. Love to God is obedience; love to God is holiness. To love God and to love man is to be conformed to the image of Christ, and this is salvation.

Moreover, faith creates peace and joy. He who has it rests, is tranquil, glad, and joyous, and this is a preparation for heaven. God gives all heavenly gifts to faith, for this reason among others, that faith works in us the life and spirit which are to be eternally manifested in the upper and better world. Faith furnishes us with armor for this life, and education for the life to come. It enables a man both to live and to die without fear; it prepares both for action and for suffering. Hence, the Lord selects it as a most convenient medium for conveying grace to us and thereby securing us for glory.

Certainly faith does for us what nothing else can

do; it gives us joy and peace, and causes us to enter into rest. Why do men attempt to gain salvation by other means? An old preacher says, "A silly servant who is told to open a door, puts his shoulder against it and pushes with all his might; but the door stirs not, and he he cannot enter, whatever strength he uses. Another comes with a key, easily unlocks the door, and enters immediately. Those who would be saved by works are pushing at heaven's gate without result, but faith is the key which opens the gate at once." Will you not use that key? The Lord commands you to believe in His dear Son. Therefore you may do so, and in doing so you shall live. Is not this the promise of the gospel, "He that believeth and is baptized shall be saved" (Mark 16:16)? What can be your objection to a way of salvation which commends itself to the mercy and the wisdom of our gracious God?

11

I Can Do Nothing!

AFTER THE ANXIOUS HEART has accepted the doctrine of atonement and learned the great truth that salvation is by faith in the Lord Jesus, it is often troubled with a sense of inability toward that which is good. Many are groaning, "I can do nothing." They are not using this as an excuse, but they feel it as a daily burden. They would if they could. They can each one honestly say, "To will is present with me; but how to perform that which is good I find not" (Ro 7:18).

This feeling seems to make all the Gospel null and void, for what is the use of food to a hungry man if he cannot get at it? Of what avail is the river of the water of life if one cannot drink? There is a story of a doctor and a poor woman's child. The sage practitioner told the mother that her little one would soon be better under proper treatment, but it was absolutely needful that her boy should regularly drink the best wine and that he should spend a season at one of the German spas. This he said to a widow who could hardly get enough bread to eat! Now, it sometimes seems to the troubled heart that the simple Gospel of "Believe and live" is not, after all, so very simple, for it asks the poor

sinner to do what he cannot do. To the really awakened
but half instructed person, there appears to be a missing
link; yonder is the salvation of Jesus, but how is it to
be reached? The soul is without strength and does
not know what to do. It lies within sight of the city of
refuge and cannot enter its gate.

Is this want of strength provided for in the plan of
salvation? It is. The work of the Lord is perfect. It
begins where we are and asks nothing of us for its
completion. When the good Samaritan saw the traveler
lying wounded and half dead, he did not tell him to rise
and come to him, mount the ass, and ride off to the inn.
No, he "came where he was" (Lk 10:33), and minis-
tered to him, and lifted him upon the beast and took
him to the inn. Thus does the Lord Jesus deal with us
in our low and wretched estate.

We have seen that God justifies, that He "justifieth
the ungodly," and that He justifies them through faith
in the precious blood of Jesus; we now have to see the
condition these ungodly ones are in when Jesus works
out their salvation. Many awakened persons are not
only troubled about their sin but about their moral
weakness. They have no strength with which to escape from the mire into which they have fallen, nor to
keep out of it in the days to come. They not only la-
ment over what they have done, but over what they
cannot do. They feel themselves to be powerless, help-
less, and spiritually lifeless. It may sound odd to say
that they feel dead, and yet it is so. They are, in their
own opinion, incapable of all good. They cannot travel
the road to heaven, for their bones are broken. "None
of the men of might [strength] have found their hands"

(Ps 76:5b). In fact, they are "without strength." Happily, it is written, as the commendation of God's love to us: "When we were yet without strength, in due time Christ died for the ungodly" (Ro 5:6).

Here we see conscious helplessness helped by the interposition of the Lord Jesus. Our helplessness is extreme. It is not written, "When we were comparatively weak Christ died for us" or, "When we had only a little strength," but the description is absolute and unrestricted: "When we were yet without strength" (Ro 5:6). We had no strength whatever which could aid in our salvation; our Lord's words were emphatically true, "Without me ye can do nothing" (Jn 15:5). I will go further than the text and remind you of the great love wherewith the Lord loved us even when we "were dead in trespasses and sins" (Eph 2:1). To be dead is even worse than being without strength.

The one thing that the poor strengthless sinner has to fix his mind upon and firmly retain as his one ground of hope is the divine assurance that "in due time Christ died for the ungodly" (Ro 5:6). Believe this, and all inability will disappear. As it is fabled of Midas that he turned everything into gold by his touch, so it is true of faith that it turns everything it touches into good. Our very needs and weaknesses become blessings when faith deals with them.

Let us consider certain forms of this lack of strength. To begin with, one man will say, "Sir, I do not seem to have the strength to collect my thoughts and keep them fixed upon those solemn topics which concern my salvation; a short prayer is almost too much for me. It is partly so, perhaps, through natural weakness, part-

ly because I have injured myself through excessive
drinking, and partly because I worry myself with
worldly cares, so that I am not capable of those high
thoughts which are necessary before a soul can be
saved."

This is a very common form of sinful weakness. Note
this! You are without strength on this point, and there
are many like you. They could not carry out a train of
consecutive thought to save their lives. Many poor men
and women are illiterate and untrained, and they find
deep thought to be very heavy work. Others are so
light and trifling by nature that they could no more
follow out a long process of argument and reasoning
than they could fly. They could never attain to the
knowledge of any profound mystery if they expended
their whole life in the effort.

You need not, therefore, despair; that which is necessary to salvation is not continuous thought but a simple
reliance upon Jesus. Hold onto this one fact: "In due
time Christ died for the ungodly." This truth will not
require from you any deep research or profound reasoning or convincing argument. There it stands: "In
due time Christ died for the ungodly." Fix your mind
on that, and rest there.

Let this one great, gracious, glorious fact lie in your
spirit till it permeates all your thoughts and makes
you rejoice, even though you are without strength, seeing that the Lord Jesus has become your strength and
your song, yea, He has become your salvation. According to the Scriptures, it is a revealed fact that in due
time Christ died for the ungodly when they were yet

without strength. Maybe, you have heard these words hundreds of times, and yet you have never before perceived their meaning. There is a wonderful thing about them. Jesus did not die for our righteousness, but He died for our sins. He did not come to save us because we were worth saving, but because we were utterly worthless, ruined, and undone. He did not come to earth out of any reason that was in us, but solely and only because of reasons which He took from the depths of His own divine love. In due time He died for those whom He describes not as godly but as *ungodly*, applying to them as hopeless an adjective as He could have selected. Even if you think little, fasten your mind to this truth, for it is fitted to the smallest capacity and is able to cheer the heaviest heart. Let this text lie under your tongue like a sweet morsel till it dissolves into your heart and flavors all your thoughts; and then it will matter very little, even though those thoughts should be as scattered as autumn leaves. Persons who have never shone in science nor displayed the least originality of thinking, have nevertheless been fully able to accept the doctrine of the cross, and have been saved. Why should not you?

I hear another man cry, "Oh, sir, my want of strength lies mainly in that I cannot repent sufficiently!" What a curious idea men have of what repentance is! Many believe that so many tears are to be shed and so many groans are to be heaved and so much despair is to be endured. Where do they get this unreasonable notion? Unbelief and despair are sins, and therefore I do not see how they can be constituent elements of acceptable repentance. Yet, there are many who regard them as necessary parts of true Christian experience. They are in great error.

Still, I know what they mean, for in the days of my darkness I used to feel the same way. I desired to repent, but I thought that I could not do it, and yet all the while I was repenting. Odd as it may sound, I felt that I could not feel. I used to get into a corner and weep because I could not weep, and I was bitterly sorrowful because I could not sorrow for sin. What a jumble it all is when in our unbelieving state we begin to judge our own condition! It is like a blind man looking at his own eyes. My heart was melted within me for fear, because I thought that my heart was as hard as an adamant stone. My heart was broken to think that it would not break. *Now* I can see that I was exhibiting the very thing which I thought I did not possess, but *then* I did not know where I was.

Oh that I could help others into the light which I now enjoy! I would gladly say a word which might shorten the time of their bewilderment. I would say a few plain words and pray "the Comforter" to apply them to the heart.

Remember that the man who truly repents is never satisfied with his own repentance. We can no more repent perfectly than we can live perfectly. However pure our tears, there will always be some dirt in them; there will be something to be repented of even in our best repentance. But listen! To repent is to change your mind about sin and Christ and all the great things of God. There is sorrow implied in this, but the main point is the turning of the heart from sin to Christ. If

there is this turning, you have the essence of true repentance, even though no alarm and no despair should
ever have cast their shadow upon your mind.

If you cannot repent as you would, it will greatly
help you to do so if you will firmly believe that "in due
time Christ died for the ungodly." Think of this again
and again. How can you continue to be hardhearted
when you know that out of supreme love "Christ died
for the ungodly"? Let me persuade you to reason with
yourself like this. Ungodly as I am, though this heart
of steel will not relent, though I hit my breast in vain,
yet He died for such as I am, because He died for the
ungodly. Oh that I may believe this and feel the power
of it upon my flinty heart!

Blot out every other reflection from your soul, and
sit down by the hour together and meditate deeply on
this one resplendent display of unmerited, unexpected,
unexampled love, "Christ died for the ungodly." Read
over carefully the narrative of the Lord's death as you
find it in the four gospels. If anything can melt your
stubborn heart, it will be the sight of the sufferings of
Jesus, and the knowledge that He suffered all this for
His enemies.

> O Jesus, sweet the tears I shed,
>   While at Thy cross I kneel,
> Gaze on Thy wounded, fainting head,
>   And all Thy sorrows feel.
> My heart dissolves to see Thee bleed,
>   This heart so hard before;
> I hear Thee for the guilty plead,
>   And grief o'erflows the more.

'Twas for the sinful Thou didst die,
    And I a sinner stand:
Convinc'd by Thine expiring eye,
    Slain by Thy piercèd hand.

RAY PALMER

Surely the cross is that wonder-working rod which
can bring water out of a rock. If you understand the
full meaning of the divine sacrifice of Jesus, you must
repent of ever having been opposed to One who is so
full of love. It is written, "They shall look upon me
whom they have pierced, and they shall mourn for
him, as one mourneth for his only son, and shall be in
bitterness for him, as one that is in bitterness for his
firstborn" (Zec 12:10). Repentance will not make you
see Christ, but to see Christ will give you repentance.
You may not make a Christ out of your repentance, but
you must look for repentance to Christ. The Holy Spirit, by turning us to Christ, turns us from sin. Look
away, then, from the effect to the cause, from your own
repenting to the Lord Jesus, who is exalted on high to
give repentance.

I have heard another say, "I am tormented with
horrible thoughts. Wherever I go, blasphemies steal
in upon me. Frequently at my work a dreadful suggestion forces itself upon me, and even on my bed I am
startled from my sleep by whispers of the evil one. I
cannot get away from this horrible temptation." Friend,
I know what you mean, for I have myself been hunted
by this wolf. A man might as well hope to fight a swarm
of flies with a sword as to master his own thoughts
when they are set on by the devil. A poor tempted
soul, assailed by satanic suggestions, is like a traveler

I have read of, about whose head and ears and whole body there came a swarm of angry bees. He could not keep them off nor escape from them. They stung him everywhere and threatened to kill him. I do not wonder that you feel that you are without strength to stop these hideous and abominable thoughts which Satan pours into your soul, but yet I would remind you of the Scripture before us, "When we were yet without strength, in due time Christ died for the ungodly."

Jesus knew where we were and where we should be; He saw that we could not overcome the prince of the power of the air. He knew that we would be greatly worried by him. But even then, when He saw us in that condition, Christ died for the ungodly. Cast the anchor of your faith upon this. The devil himself cannot tell you that you are not ungodly; believe, then, that Jesus died even for such as you are.

Remember Martin Luther's way of cutting the devil's head off with his own sword. "Oh," said the devil to Martin Luther, "you are a sinner," "Yes," said Luther, "Christ died to save sinners." Thus he smote him with his own sword. Hide in this refuge and stay there: "In due time Christ died for the ungodly." If you stand on that truth, your blasphemous thoughts which you do not have the strength to drive away will go away of themselves, for Satan will see that he is achieving nothing by plaguing you with them.

These thoughts, if you hate them, are none of yours but are injections of the devil, for which he is responsible and not you. If you strive against them, they are no more yours than are the cursings and falsehoods of rioters in the street. It is by means of these thoughts that the devil would drive you to despair, or at least keep you from trusting Jesus. The poor diseased woman could not come to Jesus because of the crowd, and you are in much the same condition because of the rush and crowd of these dreadful thoughts. Still, she put forth her finger and touched the fringe of the Lord's garment, and she was healed. Do the same.

Jesus died for those who are guilty of "all manner of sin and blasphemy," and therefore I am sure He will not refuse those who are unwillingly the captives of evil thoughts. Cast yourself upon Him, thoughts and all, and prove that He is mighty to save. He can still those horrible whisperings of the fiend, or He can enable you to see them in their true light so that you will not be worried by them. In His own way He can and will save you, and at length give you perfect peace. Only trust Him for this and everything else.

Sadly perplexing is that form of inability which lies in a supposed want of power to believe. We are not strangers to the cry:

> Oh that I could believe,
> Then all would easy be;
> I would, but cannot; Lord, relieve,
> My help must come from thee.

Many remain in the dark for years because they have no strength, they say, to give up all power and repose in the power of Another, the Lord Jesus. Indeed, this whole matter of believing is a very curious thing, for people do not get much help by trying to believe. Believing does not come by trying. If a person were to make a statement of something that happened today,

I would not tell him that I would try to believe him. If I believed in the truthfulness of the man who told me the incident and said that he saw it, I would accept the statement at once. If I did not think he was a truthful man, I would, of course, disbelieve him; but there would be no *trying* in the matter. Now, when God declares that there is salvation in Christ Jesus, I must either believe Him at once or call Him a liar. Surely you will not hesitate as to which is the right path in this case. The witness of God must be true, and we are bound at once to believe in Jesus.

But possibly you have been trying to believe too much. Do not aim at great things. Be satisfied to have a faith that can hold in its hand this one truth, "While we were yet without strength, in due time Christ died for the ungodly." He laid down His life for men while as yet they were not believing in Him, nor were able to believe in Him. He died for men, not as believers but as sinners. He came to make these sinners into believers and saints, but when He died for them He viewed them as utterly without strength. If you believe that Christ died for the ungodly, your faith will save you, and you may go in peace. If you will trust your soul to Jesus who died for the ungodly, even though you cannot believe all things or move mountains or do any other wonderful works, yet you are saved. It is not great faith but true faith that saves, and salvation lies not in the faith but in the Christ in whom faith trusts. Faith as a grain of mustard seed will bring salvation. It is not the amount of faith but the sincerity of faith which is the point to be considered. Surely a man can believe what he knows to be true; and as you know Jesus to be true, you can believe in Him.

The cross, which is the object of faith, is also, by the power of the Holy Spirit, the cause of it. Sit down and watch the dying Saviour till faith springs up spontaneously in your heart. There is no place like Calvary for creating confidence. The air of that sacred hill brings health to trembling faith. Many a watcher there has said:

> While I view Thee, wounded, grieving,
> Breathless on the cursed tree,
> Lord, I feel my heart believing
> That Thou suffer'dst thus for me.

"Alas!" cries another. "My trouble is that I cannot quit my sinning, and I know that I cannot go to heaven and carry my sin with me." I am glad that you know *that,* for it is quite true. You must be divorced from your sin or you cannot be married to Christ. Recall the question which flashed into the mind of young Bunyan while playing sports on Sunday: "Wilt thou have thy sins and go to hell, or wilt thou quit thy sins and go to heaven?" That brought him to a dead stand. That is a question which every man will have to answer, for there is no going on in sin and going to heaven. That cannot be. You must quit sin or quit hope.

Do you reply, "Yes, I am willing enough. To will is present with me, but how to perform that which I would I find not. Sin masters me, and I have no strength." Come, then, if you have no strength, this text is still true, "When we were yet without strength, in due time Christ died for the ungodly." Can you still believe *that?* However other things may seem to contradict it, will you believe it? God has said it, and it is a fact; therefore, hold on to it like grim death, for your only hope lies there. Believe this and trust Jesus, and you shall soon find power with which to slay your sin. But apart from Him, the strong man armed will hold you for ever his bondslave.

Personally, I could never have overcome my own sinfulness. I tried and failed. My evil propensities were too many for me, till, in the belief that Christ died for me, I cast my guilty soul on Him. And then I received a conquering principle by which I overcame my sinful self. The doctrine of the cross can be used to slay sin, even as the old warriors used their huge two-handed swords and mowed down their foes at every stroke. There is nothing like faith in the sinner's Friend; it overcomes all evil. If Christ has died for me, ungodly as I am, without strength as I am, then I cannot live in sin any longer but must arouse myself to love and serve Him who hath redeemed me. I cannot trifle with the evil which slew my best Friend. I must be holy for His sake. How can I live in sin when He has died to save me from it?

See what a splendid help this is to you who are without strength, to know and believe that in due time Christ died for such ungodly ones as you are. Have you caught the idea yet? It is, somehow, so difficult for our darkened, prejudiced, and unbelieving minds to see the essence of the Gospel. At times I have thought, when I have finished preaching, that I have laid down the Gospel so clearly that the nose

on one's face could not be more plain, and yet I perceive that even intelligent hearers have failed to understand what was meant by "Look unto me and be ye
saved." Converts usually say that they did not know
the Gospel till such and such a day, and yet they had
heard it for years. The Gospel is unknown, not from
want of explanation but from absence of personal revelation. This the Holy Spirit is ready to give and will
give to those who ask Him. Yet, when given, the sum
total of the truth revealed all lies within these words:
"Christ died for the ungodly."

I hear another person bewailing himself thus: "Oh,
sir, my weakness lies in this, that I do not seem to keep
spiritual things long in my mind! I hear the Word on
a Sunday, and I am impressed; but in the week I meet
with an evil companion, and my good feelings are all
gone. My fellow workmen do not believe in anything,
and they say such terrible things. I do not know how
to answer them, so I find myself knocked over." I know
this Plastic Pliable very well, and I tremble for him;
but at the same time, if he is really sincere, his weakness can be met by divine grace. The Holy Spirit can
cast out the evil spirit of the fear of man. He can make
the coward brave.

Remember, my poor vacillating friend, you must not
remain in this state. It will never do to be mean and
beggarly to yourself. Stand upright and look at yourself, and see if you were ever meant to be like a toad
under a harrow, afraid for your life either to move or
to stand still. Do have a mind of your own.

This is not a spiritual matter only, but one which concerns ordinary manliness. I would do many things to

please my friends, but to go to hell to please them is more than I would venture. It may be very well to do this and that for good fellowship, but it will never do to lose the friendship of God in order to keep on good terms with men. "I know that," says the man, "but still, though I know it, I cannot get enough courage. I cannot show my colors. I cannot stand fast." Well, to you also I have the same text to bring: "When we were yet without strength, in due time Christ died for the ungodly."

If Peter were here, he would say, "The Lord Jesus died for me even when I was such a poor weak creature that the maid who kept the fire drove me to lie, and to swear that I knew not the Lord." Yes, Jesus died for those who forsook Him and fled. Take a firm grip on this truth: Christ died for the ungodly while they were yet without strength. This is your way out of your cowardice. Get this worked into your soul, "Christ died for me," and you will soon be ready to die for Him. Believe that He suffered in your place and stead and offered for you a full, true, and satisfactory expiation. If you believe that fact, you will be forced to feel, "I cannot be ashamed of Him who died for me." A full conviction that this is true will give you dauntless courage.

Look at the saints in the martyr age. In the early days of Christianity, when this great thought of Christ's exceeding love was sparkling in all its freshness in the Church, men were not only ready to die, but they grew ambitious to suffer and even presented themselves by hundreds at the judgment seats of the rulers, confessing the Christ. I do not say that they were wise to court a cruel death, but it proves my point that a sense of the love of Jesus lifts the mind above all fear of what man can do to us. Why should it not produce the same effect in you? Oh that it might now inspire you with a brave resolve to come out upon the Lord's side and be His follower to the end!

May the Holy Spirit help us to come thus far by faith in the Lord Jesus, and it will be well!

12

The Increase of Faith

How CAN WE OBTAIN an increase of faith? This is a very earnest question to many. They say they want to believe but cannot. A great deal of nonsense is said about this subject. Let us be strictly practical in our dealing with it. Common sense is as much needed in religion as anywhere else. "What am I to do in order to believe?" One who was asked the best way to do a certain simple act, replied that the best way to do it was to do it at once. We waste time in discussing methods when the action is simple. The shortest way to believe is to believe. If the Holy Spirit has made you candid, you will believe as soon as truth is set before you. You will believe it because it is true. The Gospel command is clear, "Believe on the Lord Jesus Christ, and thou shalt be saved" (Ac 16:31). It is idle to evade this by questions and quibbles. The order is plain; let it be obeyed.

But still, if you have difficulty, take it before God in prayer. Tell God the Father exactly what it is that puzzles you, and beg Him by His Holy Spirit to solve the question. If I cannot believe a statement in a book, I inquire of the author what he means by it; and if he is a true man, his explanation will satisfy me. Much more will the divine explanation of the hard points of Scripture satisfy the heart of the true seeker. The Lord is willing to make Himself known; go to Him and see if it is not so. Go at once to your closet and cry, "O Holy Spirit, lead me into the truth! What I know not, teach Thou me."

Furthermore, if faith seems difficult, it is possible that God the Holy Spirit will enable you to believe if you hear very frequently and earnestly that which you are commanded to believe. We believe many things because we have heard them so often. Do you not find it so in everyday life that if you hear a thing fifty times a day, at last you come to believe it? Some men have come to believe very unlikely statements by this process, and therefore I do not wonder that the Holy Spirit often blesses the method of often hearing the truth and uses it to work faith concerning that which is to be believed. It is written, "Faith cometh by hearing"; therefore, hear often. If I earnestly and attentively hear the Gospel, one of these days I shall find myself believing that which I hear because of the blessed operation of the Spirit of God upon my mind. Only be sure you hear the Gospel, and do not distract your mind with either hearing or reading that which is designed to stagger you.

If that, however, should seem to be poor advice, I would add next, consider the testimony of others. The Samaritans believed because of what the woman told them concerning Jesus. Many of our beliefs arise out of the testimony of others. I believe that there is such a country as Japan; I never have seen it, and yet I believe that there is such a place because others have been there. I believe that I shall die; I have never died, but a great many people whom I once knew have died, and therefore I have a conviction that I shall die also. The testimony of many convinces me of that fact.

Listen, then, to those who tell you how they were saved, how they were pardoned, how they were changed in character. If you will look into the matter you will find that somebody just like yourself has been saved. If you have been a thief, you will find that a thief rejoiced to wash away his sin in the fountain of Christ's blood. If unhappily you have been unchaste, you will find that men and women who have fallen in that way have been cleansed and changed. If you are in despair, you only need to get among God's people and inquire a little, and you will discover that some of the saints have been equally in despair at times and they will be pleased to tell you how the Lord delivered them. As you listen to one after another of those who have tried the Word of God and proved it, the divine Spirit will lead you to believe.

Have you heard of the African who was told by the missionary that water sometimes becomes so hard that a man could walk on it? He declared that he believed a great many things the missionary had told him, but he would never believe that. When he came to England he saw the river frozen one frosty day, but he would not walk on it. He knew that it was a deep river, and he felt certain that he would be drowned if he walked on it. He could not be induced to walk on the frozen water till his friend and many others went on it; then he was persuaded and trusted himself where others had

safely walked. So, when you see others believe in the
Lamb of God and notice their joy and peace, you will
yourself be gently led to believe. The experience of
others is one of God's ways of helping us to faith. You
have either to believe in Jesus or die; there is no hope
for you but in Him.

A better plan is this: Note the authority upon which
you are commanded to believe, and this will greatly
help you to faith. The authority is not mine, or you
might well reject it. But you are commanded to believe upon the authority of God Himself. *He* bids you
to believe in Jesus Christ, and you must not refuse to
obey your Maker. The foreman of a certain factory had
often heard the Gospel, but he was troubled with the
fear that he might not come to Christ. His employer
one day sent a card to the factory; "Come to my house
immediately after work." The foreman appeared at his
employer's door, and the employer came out and said
somewhat roughly, "What do you want, John, trou-
bling me at this time? Work is done; what right have
you here?" "Sir," he said, "I had a card from you saying that I was to come after work." "Do you mean to
say that merely because you had a card from me you
came to my house and called me out after business
hours?" "Well, sir," replied the foreman, "I do not
understand you, but it seems to me that since you
sent for me, I had a right to come." "Come in, John,"
said his employer, "I have another message that I want
to read to you," and he sat down and read these words:
"Come unto me, all ye that labour and are heavy
laden, and I will give you rest" (Mt 11:28). "Do you
think after such a message from Christ that you can

be wrong in coming to Him?" The poor man saw it all
at once, and believed in the Lord Jesus for eternal life,
because he perceived that he had good warrant and
authority for believing. So have you! You have good
authority for comng to Christ, for the Lord Himself
tells you to trust Him.

If that does not bring about faith in you, think over
what it is that you have to believe—that the Lord Jesus
Christ suffered in the place and stead of sinners, and
is able to save all who trust Him. Why, this is the most
blessed fact that ever men were told to believe; it is
the most suitable, the most comforting, the most divine
truth that was ever set before mortal minds. I advise
you to think much upon it, and search out the grace
and love which it contains. Study the four gospels,
study Paul's epistles, and then see if the message is not
such a credible one that you are forced to believe it.

If that does not do, then think upon the person of
Jesus Christ—think of *who* He is and *what* He did and
where He is and *what* He is. How can you doubt *Him?*
It is cruelty to distrust the ever truthful Jesus. He has
done nothing to deserve distrust; on the contrary, it
should be easy to rely upon Him. Why crucify Him
anew by unbelief? Is not this crowning Him with
thorns again, and spitting upon Him again? What! Is
he not to be trusted? What worse insult did the soldiers
pour upon Him than this? They made Him a martyr,
but you make Him a liar, which is far worse. Do not
ask, *How can I believe?* But answer another question: *How can you disbelieve?*

If none of these things avail, then there is something wrong about you altogether, and my last word

is, submit yourself to God! Prejudice or pride is at the bottom of this unbelief. May the Spirit of God take away your enmity and make you yield. You are a rebel, a proud rebel, and that is why you do not believe your God. Give up your rebellion; throw down your weapons. Yield at discretion; surrender to your King. I believe that never did a soul throw up its hands in self-despair and cry, "Lord, I yield," but what faith became easy to it before long. It is because you still have a quarrel with God and resolve to have your own will and your own way that therefore you cannot believe. "How can ye believe," said Christ, "which receive honour one of another . . . ?" (Jn 5:44). Proud self creates unbelief. Submit. Yield to your God, and then shall you sweetly believe in your Saviour. May the Holy Spirit now work secretly but effectually with you and bring you at this very moment to believe in the Lord Jesus! Amen.

13

Regeneration and the Holy Spirit

YE MUST BE BORN AGAIN." This word of our Lord Jesus has appeared to flame in the way of many, like the drawn sword of the cherub at the gate of paradise. They have despaired because this change is beyond their utmost effort. The new birth is from above, and therefore it is not in the creature's power. Now, it is far from my mind to deny or ever to conceal a truth in order to create a false comfort. I freely admit that the new birth is supernatural, and that it cannot be done by the sinner's own self. It would be a poor help to you if I were wicked enough to try to cheer you by persuading you to reject or forget what is unquestionably true.

But is it not remarkable that the very chapter in which our Lord makes this sweeping declaration also contains the most explicit statement as to salvation by faith? Read chapter 3 of John's Gospel and do not dwell alone upon its earlier sentences. It is true that verse 3 says: "Jesus answered and said unto him, Verily, verily, I say unto thee, Except a man be born again, he cannot see the kingdom of God."

But, then, verses 14 and 15 say: "And as Moses lifted

up the serpent in the wilderness, even so must the Son
of man be lifted up: that whosover believeth in him
should not perish, but have eternal life."

Verse 18 repeats the same doctrine in the broadest
terms: "He that believeth on him is not condemned:
but he that believeth not is condemned already, because he hath not believed in the name of the only
begotten Son of God."

It is clear that these two statements must agree since
they came from the same lips and are recorded on the
same inspired page. Why should we find difficulty
where there can be none? If one statement assures us
of the necessity to salvation of something which only
God can give, and if another assures us that the Lord
will save us upon our believing in Jesus, then we may
safely conclude that the Lord will give to those who
believe all that is declared to be necessary to salvation.
The Lord does, in fact, produce the new birth in all
who believe in Jesus, and their believing is the surest
evidence that they are born again.

We trust in Jesus for what we cannot do ourselves.
If it were in our own power, why would we need to
look to Him? It is ours to believe; it is the Lord's to
create us anew. He will not believe for us; neither
are we to do regenerating work for Him. It is enough
for us to obey the gracious command; it is for the Lord
to work the new birth in us. He who could go so far as
to die on the cross for us, can and will give us all things
that are needful for our eternal safety.

"But a saving change of heart is the work of the
Holy Spirit." This also is most true, and let it be far
from us to question it or to forget it. But the work of

the Holy Spirit is secret and mysterious, and it can only be perceived by its results. There are mysteries about our natural birth into which it would be an unhallowed curiosity to pry; still more is this the case with the sacred operations of the Spirit of God. "The wind bloweth where it listeth, and thou hearest the sound thereof, but canst not tell whence it cometh, and whither it goeth; so is every one that is born of the Spirit" (Jn 3:8). This much, however, we do know—the mysterious work of the Holy Spirit cannot be a reason for refusing to believe in Jesus to whom that same Spirit beareth witness.

If a man were told to sow a field, he could not excuse his neglect by saying that it would be useless to sow unless God caused the seed to grow. He would not be justified in neglecting tillage because the secret energy of God alone can create a harvest. No one is hindered in the ordinary pursuits of life by the fact that unless the Lord build the house they labor in vain that build it. It is certain that no man who believes in Jesus will ever find that the Holy Spirit refuses to work in him; in fact, his believing is the proof that the Spirit is already at work in his heart.

God works in providence, but men do not therefore sit still. They could not move without the divine power giving them life and strength, and yet they proceed upon their way without question, the power being bestowed from day to day by Him in whose hand their breath is, and whose are all their ways. So is it in grace. We repent and believe, though we could do neither if the Lord did not enable us. We forsake sin and trust in Jesus, and then we perceive that the Lord has caused us to will and to do of His own good pleasure. It is idle to pretend that there is any real difficulty in the matter.

Some truths which are hard to explain in words are simple enough in actual experience. There is no discrepancy between the truth that the sinner believes and that his faith is wrought in him by the Holy Spirit. Only folly can lead men to puzzle themselves about plain matters while their souls are in danger. No man would refuse to enter a lifeboat because he did not know the specific gravity of bodies; neither would a starving man decline to eat till he understood the whole process of nutrition. If you will not believe till you can understand all mysteries, you will never be saved at all; and if you allow self-invented difficulties to keep you from accepting pardon through your Lord and Saviour, you will perish in a condemnation which will be richly deserved. Do not commit spiritual suicide through a passion for discussing metaphysical subtleties.

14

"My Redeemer Liveth"

I HAVE SPOKEN CONTINUALLY to you concerning Christ crucified, who is the great hope of the guilty, but we will be wise to remember that our Lord has risen from the dead and lives eternally.

You are not asked to trust in a dead Jesus but in One who, though He died for our sins, has risen again for our justification. You may go to Jesus at once as to a living and present friend. He is not a mere memory but a continually existent Person who will hear your prayers and answer them. He lives on purpose to carry on the work for which He once laid down His life. He is interceding for sinners at the right hand of the Father, and for this reason He is able to save them to the uttermost who come unto God by Him. Come and try this living Saviour if you have never done so before.

This living Jesus is also raised to an eminence of glory and power. He does not now sorrow as "a humble man before his foes," nor labor as "the carpenter's son," but He is exalted far above principalities and power and every name that is named. The Father has given Him all power in heaven and in earth, and He exercises this high endowment in carrying out His work of grace.

Hear what Peter and the other apostles testified concerning Him before the high priest and the council.

> The God of our fathers raised up Jesus, whom ye slew and hanged on a tree. Him hath God exalted with his right hand to be a Prince and a Saviour, for to give repentance to Israel, and forgiveness of sins (Ac 5:30-31).

The glory which surrounds the ascended Lord should breathe hope into every believer's breast. Jesus is no mean person; He is "a Saviour and a great one." He is the crowned and enthroned Redeemer of men. The sovereign prerogative of life and death is vested in Him; the Father has put all men under the mediatorial government of the Son so that He can quicken whom He will. He openeth and no man shutteth. At His word the soul which is bound by the cords of sin and condemnation can be unloosed in a moment. He stretches out the silver scepter, and whosoever touches it lives.

It is well for us that as sin lives and the flesh lives and the devil lives, so Jesus lives; and it is also well that whatever might these may have to ruin us, Jesus has still greater power to save us.

All His exaltation and ability are on our account. "He is exalted *to be*" and exalted "*to give*." He is exalted to be a Prince and a Saviour that He may give all that is needed to accomplish the salvation of all who come under His rule. Jesus *has* nothing which He will not use for a sinner's salvation, and He *is* nothing which He will not display in the abundance of His grace. He links His princedom with His Saviourship, as if He would not have the one without the other; and He sets forth His exaltation as designed to bring blessings to men, as if this were the flower and crown of His glory. Could anything be more calculated to raise the hopes of seeking sinners who are looking Christward?

Jesus endured great humiliation, and therefore there was room for Him to be exalted. By that humiliation He accomplished and endured all the Father's will, and therefore He was rewarded by being raised to glory. He uses that exaltation on behalf of His people. Raise your eyes to these hills of glory, from where your help must come. Contemplate the high glories of the Prince and Savour. Is it not most hopeful for men that a Man is now on the throne of the universe? Is it not glorious that the Lord of all is the Saviour of sinners? We have a Friend at court; yea, a Friend on the throne. He will use all His influence for those who entrust their affairs in His hands. Well does one of our poets sing:

> He ever lives to intercede
>   Before His Father's face;
> Give Him, my soul, Thy cause to plead,
>   No doubt the Father's grace.

Come and commit your cause and your case to those once-pierced hands which are now glorified with the signet rings of royal power and honor. No suit ever failed which was left with this great Advocate.

15

Repentance Must Go with Forgiveness

IT IS CLEAR from the text which we quoted earlier that repentance is bound up with the forgiveness of sins. In Acts 5:31 we read that Jesus is exalted to give repentance and forgiveness of sins. These two blessings come from that sacred hand which once was nailed to the tree but is now raised to glory. Repentance and forgiveness are riveted together by the eternal purpose of God. What God hath joined together let no man put asunder.

Repentance must go with remission, and you will see that it is so if you think a little about the matter. It cannot be that pardon of sin should be given to an impenitent sinner; this would be to confirm him in his evil ways, and to teach him to think little of evil. If the Lord were to say, "You love sin and live in it, and you are going on from bad to worse, but all the same, I forgive you," this would proclaim a horrible license for iniquity. The foundations of social order would be removed, and moral anarchy would follow. I cannot tell what innumerable wrongs would certainly occur

94

if you could divide repentance and forgiveness, and pass by the sin while the sinner remained as fond of it as ever.

In the very nature of things, if we believe in the holiness of God it must be that if we continue in our sin and will not repent of it, we cannot be forgiven but must reap the consequence of our obstinancy. According to the infinite goodness of God, we are promised that if we will forsake our sins, confessing them, and will by faith accept the grace which is provided in Christ Jesus, God "is faithful and just to forgive us our sins, and to cleanse us from all unrighteousness" (1 Jn 1:9). But, as long as God lives, there can be no promise of mercy to those who continue in their evil ways and refuse to acknowledge their wrongdoing. Surely no rebel can expect the King to pardon his treason while he remains in open revolt. No one can be so foolish as to imagine that the Judge of all the earth will put away our sins if we refuse to put them away ourselves.

Moreover, it must be so for the completeness of divine mercy. That mercy which could forgive the sin and yet let the sinner live in it would be scant and superficial mercy. It would be unequal and deformed mercy, lame in one foot, and withered in one of its hands. Which do you think is the greater privilege: cleansing from the guilt of sin, or deliverance from the power of sin? I will not attempt to weigh in the scales two mercies so surpassing. Neither of them could have come to us apart from the precious blood of Jesus. But it seems to me that to be delivered from the dominion of sin and to be made holy, to be made like God must

be reckoned as the greater of the two, if a comparison
has to be drawn.

To be forgiven is an immeasurable favor. We make
this one of the first notes of our psalm of praise: "Who
forgiveth all thine iniquities" (Ps 103:3). But if we
could be forgiven and then could be permitted to love
sin, to riot in iniquity, and to wallow in lust, what
would be the use of such a forgiveness? Might it not
turn out to be poisoned candy which would most effectually destroy us? To be washed and yet to lie in the
mire, to be pronounced clean and yet to have the lep-
rosy white on one's brow, that would be the worst
mockery of mercy. What good is it to bring the man
out of his sepulcher if you leave him dead? Why lead
him into the light if he is still blind?

We thank God that He who forgives our iniquities
also heals our diseases. He who washes us from the
stains of the past also uplifts us from the foul ways of
the present and keeps us from falling in the future. We
must joyfully accept both repentance and remission;
they cannot be separated. The covenant heritage is
one and indivisible and must not be parceled out. To
divide the work of grace would be to cut the living
child in half, and those who would permit this have
no interest in it.

You who are seeking the Lord, would you be satisfied with one of these mercies alone? Would you be
content if God would forgive you your sin and then
allow you to be as worldly and wicked as before? Oh,
no! The quickened spirit is more afraid of sin itself
than of the penal results of it. The cry of your heart
is not, "Who shall deliver me from punishment?" but,

"O wretched man that I am! Who shall deliver me from the body of this death?" (Ro 7:24). "Who shall enable me to live above temptation and to become holy, even as God is holy?" Since the unity of repentance with remission agrees with gracious desire, and since it is necessary for the completeness of salvation, and for holiness' sake, rest assured that it abides.

Repentance and forgiveness are joined together in the experience of all believers. There never was a person who did unfeignedly repent of sin with believing repentance who was not forgiven. On the other hand, there never was a person forgiven who had not repented of his sin. I do not hesitate to say that beneath heaven there never was, there is not, and there never will be any case of sin being washed away unless at the same time the heart was led to repentance and faith in Christ. Hatred of sin and a sense of pardon come together into the soul, and abide together while we live.

These two things act and react upon each other. The man who is forgiven, therefore repents; and the man who repents is also most assuredly forgiven. Remember first, that forgiveness leads to repentance. As we sing in Hart's words:

> Law and terrors do but harden,
> All the while they work alone;
> But a sense of blood-bought pardon
> Soon dissolves a heart of stone.

When we are sure that we are forgiven, then we abhor iniquity. And I suppose that when faith grows into full assurance, so that we are certain beyond a doubt that the blood of Jesus has washed us whiter than snow, it is then that repentance reaches to its greatest height. Repentance grows as faith grows. Do not make any mistake about it; repentance is not a thing of days and weeks, a temporary penance to be got over as fast as possible! No, it is the grace of a lifetime, like faith itself. God's little children repent, and so do the young men and the fathers. Repentance is the inseparable companion of faith. All the while that we walk by faith and not by sight, the tear of repentance glitters in the eye of faith. That is not true repentance which does not come of faith in Jesus, and that is not true faith in Jesus which is not tinctured with repentance. Faith and repentance, like Siamese twins, are vitally joined together. In proportion as we believe in the forgiving love of Christ, in that proportion we repent; and in proportion as we repent of sin and hate evil, we rejoice in the fullness of the absolution which Jesus is exalted to bestow. You will never value pardon unless you feel repentance, and you will never taste the deepest draught of repentance until you know that you are pardoned. It may seem a strange thing and so it is; the bitterness of repentance and the sweetness of pardon blend in the flavor of every gracious life, and make up an incomparable happiness.

These two covenant gifts are the mutual assurance of each other. If I know that I repent, I know that I am forgiven. How am I to know that I am forgiven except I know also that I am turned from my former sinful course? To be a believer is to be a penitent. Faith and repentance are but two spokes in the same wheel, two handles of the same plow. Repentance has been well described as a heart broken *for* sin and *from* sin, and it may equally well be spoken of as turning and returning. It is a change of mind of the most thorough and radical sort, and it is attended with sorrow for the past and a resolve of amendment in the future.

> Repentance is to leave
>   The sins we loved before;
> And show that we in earnest grieve,
>   By doing so no more.

Now, when that is the case, we may be certain that we are forgiven, for the Lord never made a heart to be broken for sin and broken from sin without pardoning it. If on the other hand, we are enjoying pardon through the blood of Jesus and are justified by faith and have peace with God through Jesus Christ our Lord, we know that our repentance and faith are of the right sort.

Do not regard your repentance as the cause of your remission, but as the companion of it. Do not expect to be able to repent until you see the grace of our Lord Jesus and His readiness to blot out your sin. Keep these blessed things in their places, and view them in their relation to each other. They are the Jachin and Boaz of a saving experience. I mean that they are comparable to Solomon's two great pillars which stood in the forefront of the house of the Lord, and formed a majestic entrance to the holy place. No man comes to God aright unless he passes between the pillars of repentance and remission. Upon your heart the rainbow of covenant grace has been displayed in all its beauty

when the teardrops of repentance have been shone
upon by the light of full forgiveness. Repentance of
sin and faith in divine pardon are the warp and woof
of the fabric of real conversion. By these tokens shall
you know an Israelite indeed.

To come back to the Scripture upon which we are
meditating: both forgiveness and repentance flow from
the same source and are given by the same Saviour.
The Lord Jesus in His glory bestows both upon the
same persons. You can find neither the remission nor
the repentance elsewhere. Jesus has both ready, and
He is prepared to bestow them now and to bestow them
most freely on all who will accept them at His hands.
Let it never be forgotten that Jesus gives all that is
needful for our salvation. It is highly important that
all seekers after mercy should remember this. Faith is
as much the gift of God as is the Saviour upon whom
that faith relies. Repentance of sin is as truly the work
of grace as the making of an atonement by which sin
is blotted out. Salvation, from first to last, is of grace
alone. Do not misunderstand me. It is not the Holy
Spirit who repents. He has never done anything for
which He should repent. If He could repent, it would
not help us. We ourselves must repent of our own sin,
or we are not saved from its power. It is not the Lord
Jesus Christ who repents. What should He repent of?
We ourselves repent with the full consent of every
faculty of our mind. The will, the affections, and the
emotions all work together most heartily in the blessed
act of repentance for sin. And yet, at the back of all
which is our personal act, there is a secret holy influence which melts the heart, gives contrition, and pro-

duces a complete change. The Spirit of God enlightens us to see what sin is and thus makes it loathsome in our eyes. The Spirit of God also turns us toward holiness, makes us greatly to appreciate, love, and desire it, and thus gives us the impetus by which we are led onward from stage to stage of sanctification. The Spirit of God works in us to will and to do according to God's good pleasure. To that good Spirit let us submit ourselves at once so that He may lead us to Jesus, who will freely give us the double benediction of repentance and remission, according to the riches of His grace. "By grace are ye saved" (Eph 2:8).

16

How Repentance Is Given

RETURN to the grand text: "Him hath God exalted with his right hand to be a Prince and a Saviour, for to give repentance to Israel, and forgiveness of sins." Our Lord Jesus Christ has gone up that grace may come down. His glory is employed to give greater currency to His grace. The Lord has not taken a step upward except with the design of bearing believing sinners upward with Him. He is exalted to give repentance, and this we shall see if we remember a few great truths.

The work which our Lord Jesus has done has made repentance possible, available, and acceptable. The Law makes no mention of repentance, but says plainly, "The soul that sinneth, it shall die" (Eze 18:20). If the Lord Jesus had not died and risen again and gone unto the Father, what would your repenting or mine be worth? We might feel remorse with its horrors, but never repentance with its hopes. Repentance, as a natural feeling, is a common duty deserving no great praise. Indeed, it is so generally mingled with a selfish fear of punishment that the kindest estimate makes little of it. Had not Jesus interposed and accomplished a wealth of merit, our tears of repentance would have been so much water spilled upon the ground. Jesus is exalted on high so that through the virtue of His intercession, repentance may have a place before God. In this respect He gives us repentance, because He puts repentance into a position of acceptance which otherwise it could never have occupied.

When Jesus was exalted on high, the Spirit of God was poured out to work all needful graces in us. The Holy Spirit creates repentance in us by supernaturally renewing our nature and taking the heart of stone out of our flesh. Oh, do not sit down straining those eyes of yours to make impossible tears! Repentance comes not from an unwilling nature, but from free and sovereign grace. Do not go to your room to smite your breast in order to bring from a heart of stone feelings which are not there. But go to Calvary and see how Jesus died. Look upward to the hills from where your help comes. The Holy Spirit has come on purpose that He may overshadow men's spirits and breed repentance within them, even as once He brooded over chaos and brought forth order. Breathe your prayer to Him, "Blessed Spirit, dwell with me. Make me tender and lowly of heart that I may hate sin and unfeignedly repent of it." He will hear your cry and answer you.

Remember, too, that when our Lord Jesus was exalted, He not only gave us repentance by sending forth the Holy Spirit, but by consecrating all the works of nature and of providence to the great ends of our salvation, so that any one of them may call us to repentance, whether it crow like Peter's cock or shake the prison like the jailer's earthquake. From the right hand of God our Lord Jesus rules all things here below and

makes them work together for the salvation of His
redeemed. He uses both bitter and sweet things, trials
and joys, that He may produce in sinners a better mind
toward their God. Be thankful for the providence
which has made you poor or sick or sad, for by all this
Jesus works the life of your spirit and turns you to
Himself. The Lord's mercy often rides to the door of
our hearts on the black horse of affliction. Jesus uses
the whole range of our experience to wean us from
earth and woo us to heaven. Christ is exalted to the
throne of heaven and earth in order that, by all the
processes of His providence, He may subdue hard
hearts unto the gracious softening of repentance.

Besides, He is at work at this hour by all His whispers in the conscience, by His inspired Book, by those
of us who speak out of that Book, and by praying
friends and earnest hearts. He can send a word to you
which shall strike your rocky heart as with the rod of
Moses and cause streams of repentance to flow forth.
He can bring to your mind some heartbreaking text
out of Holy Scripture which shall conquer you immediately. He can mysteriously soften you and cause a
holy frame of mind to steal over you when you least
look for it. Be sure of this, that He who is gone into
His glory, raised into all the splendor and majesty of
God, has abundant ways of working repentance in
those to whom He grants forgiveness. He is even now
waiting to give repentance to you. Ask Him for it at
once.

Observe with great comfort that the Lord Jesus
Christ gives this repentance to the most unlikely people in the world. He is exalted to give repentance to

Israel. To Israel! In the days when the apostles thus spoke, Israel was the nation which had most grossly sinned against light and love by daring to say, "His blood be on us, and on our children" (Mt 27:25). Yet Jesus is exalted to give *them* repentance! What a marvel of grace! If you have been brought up in the brightest of Christian light and yet have rejected it, there is still hope. If you have sinned against conscience and against the Holy Spirit and against the love of Jesus, there is still room for repentance. Though you may be as hard as unbelieving Israel of old, softening may yet come to you, since Jesus is exalted and clothed with boundless power. For those who went the furthest in iniquity and sinned with special aggravation, the Lord Jesus is exalted to give to them repentance and forgiveness of sins. I am happy to have so full a Gospel to proclaim! Happy are you to be allowed to read it!

The hearts of the children of Israel had grown as hard as an adamant stone. Luther used to think it impossible to convert a Jew. We are far from agreeing with him, and yet we must admit that the seed of Israel have been exceedingly obstinate in their rejection of the Saviour during these many centuries. Truly did the Lord say, "Israel would none of me" (Ps 81:11). "He came unto his own, and his own received him not" (Jn 1:11). Yet on behalf of Israel our Lord Jesus is exalted for the giving of repentance and remission. Probably you are a Gentile, but yet you may have a very stubborn heart which has stood against the Lord Jesus for many years; and yet our Lord can work repentance in you. It may be that you

will feel compelled to write as William Hone did when
he yielded to divine love. He was the author of some
entertaining volumes called the "Everyday Book," but
he was once an out-and-out atheist. When subdued
by sovereign grace, he wrote:

> The proudest heart that ever beat
>   Hath been subdued in me;
> The wildest will that ever rose
> To scorn Thy cause and aid Thy foes
>   Is quell'd my Lord, by Thee.
> Thy will, and not my will be done,
>   My heart be ever Thine;
> Confessing Thee the mighty Word,
> My Saviour Christ, my God, my Lord,
>   Thy cross shall be my sign.

The Lord can give repentance to the most unlikely,
turning lions into lambs, and ravens into doves. Let us
look to Him that this great change may take place in
us. Assuredly the contemplation of the death of Christ
is one of the surest and speediest methods of gaining
repentance. Do not sit down and try to pump up repentance from the dry well of a corrupt nature. It is
contrary to the laws of your mind to suppose that you
can force your soul into that gracious state. Take your
heart in prayer to Him who understands it, and say,
"Lord, cleanse it. Lord, renew it. Lord, work repentance in it." The more you try to produce penitent emotions in yourself, the more you will be disappointed;
but if you believingly think of Jesus dying for you, repentance will burst forth. Meditate on the Lord's
shedding His heart's blood out of love to you. Set be-

fore your mind's eye the agony and bloody sweat, the cross and passion. And, as you do this, He who was the Bearer of all this grief will look at you, and with that look He will do for you what He did for Peter, so that you also will go out and weep bitterly. He who died for you can, by His gracious Spirit, make you die to sin; and He who has gone into glory on your behalf can draw your soul after Him, away from evil and toward holiness.

I shall be content if I leave this one thought with you; look not beneath the ice to find fire, neither hope in your own natural heart to find repentance. Look to the living One for life. Look to Jesus for all you need between the gate of hell and the gate of heaven. Never seek elsewhere for any part of that which Jesus loves to bestow, but remember, Christ is all.

17

The Fear of Final Falling

A DARK FEAR haunts the minds of many who are coming to Christ; they are afraid that they shall not persevere to the end. I have heard the seeker say, "If I were to cast my soul upon Jesus, yet perhaps I would after all draw back into perdition. I have had good feelings before now, and they have died away. My goodness has been as the morning cloud and as the early dew. It has come suddenly, lasted for a season, promised much, and then vanished away."

I believe that this fear is often the father of the fact, and that some who have been afraid to trust Christ for all time and for all eternity have failed because they had a temporary faith which never went far enough to save them. They set out trusting to Jesus in a measure, but looking to themselves for continuance and perseverance in the heavenward way; and so they set out faultily, and, as a natural consequence, turned back before long. If we trust to ourselves for our holding on we shall *not* hold on. Even though we rest in Jesus for a part of our salvation, we shall fail if we trust to self for anything. No chain is stronger than its weakest link. If Jesus be our hope for everything except one thing, we shall utterly fail because in that one point we shall come to nothing. I have no doubt whatever that a mistake about the perseverance of the saints has prevented the perseverance of many who did run well. What did hinder them that they should not continue to run? They trusted to themselves for that running, and so they stopped short. Beware of mixing even a little of self with the mortar with which you build, or you will make it untempered mortar, and the stones will not hold together. If you look to Christ for your beginning, beware of looking to yourself for your ending. He is Alpha. See to it that you make Him Omega also. If you begin in the Spirit you must not hope to be made perfect by the flesh. Begin as you mean to go on, and go on as you began, and let the Lord be all in all to you. Oh, that God the Holy Spirit may give us a very clear idea of where the strength must come from by which we shall be preserved until the day of our Lord's appearing!

Here is what Paul said upon this subject when he was writing to the Corinthians:

> Our Lord Jesus Christ: who shall also confirm you unto the end, that ye may be blameless in the day of our Lord Jesus Christ. God is faithful, by whom ye were called unto the fellowship of his Son Jesus Christ our Lord (1 Co 1:7-9).

This language silently admits a great need by telling us how it is provided for. Wherever the Lord makes a provision, we are quite sure that there was a need for it, since no superfluities encumber the covenant of grace. Golden shields which hung in Solomon's courts

were never used, but there are none such in the armory
of God. What God has provided we shall surely need.
Between this hour and the consummation of all things,
every promise of God and every provision of the covenant of grace will be brought into requisition. The
urgent need of the believing soul is confirmation, continuance, final perseverance, preservation to the end.
This is the great necessity of the most advanced believers, for Paul was writing to saints at Corinth who
were men of a high order, of whom he could say, "I
thank my God always on your behalf, for the grace of
God which is given you by Jesus Christ" (1 Co 1:4).

Such men are the very persons who most assuredly
feel that they have daily need of new grace if they are
to hold on and hold out and become conquerors at the
last. If you were not saints you would have no grace,
and you would feel no need of more grace; but because
you are men of God, therefore you feel the daily demands of the spiritual life. The marble statue requires
no food; but the living man hungers and thirsts, and
he rejoices that his bread and his water are guaranteed
for him, or else he would certainly faint by the way.
The believer's personal wants make it inevitable that
he should daily draw from the great source of all sup-
plies, for what could he do if he could not resort to
his God?

This is true of the most gifted of the saints, of those
men at Corinth who were enriched with all utterance
and with all knowledge. They needed to be confirmed
to the end, or else their gifts and attainments would
prove their ruin. If we had the tongues of men and
of angels, if we did not receive fresh grace, where

would we be? If we had all experience till we were
fathers in the Church—if we had been taught of God so
as to understand all mysteries—yet we could not live a
single day without the divine life flowing into us from
our covenant Head. How could we hope to hold on
for a single hour, to say nothing of a lifetime, unless
the Lord should hold onto us? He who began the good
work in us must perform it unto the day of Christ, or it
will prove a painful failure.

This great necessity arises very much from our own
selves. In some there is a painful fear that they shall
not persevere in grace because they know their own
fickleness. Certain persons are constitutionally unstable.
Some men are by nature conservative, not to say obstinate, but others are as naturally variable and volatile. Like butterflies they flit from flower to flower till
they visit all the beauties of the garden and settle upon
none of them. They are never long enough in one
place to do any good, not even in their business nor
in their intellectual pursuits. Such persons may well
be afraid that ten, twenty, thirty, forty, perhaps fifty
years of continuous religious watchfulness will be a
great deal too much for them. We see men joining first
one church and then another, till they have tried them
all. They are everything by turn and nothing long.
Such have double need to pray that they may be di-
vinely confirmed, and may be made not only steadfast
but unmovable, or otherwise they will not be found
"always abounding in the work of the Lord" (1 Co 15:
58).

All of us, even if we have no constitutional temptation to fickleness, must feel our own weakness if we

are really quickened of God. Do you not find enough in
any one single day to make you stumble? You that desire to walk in perfect holiness, as I trust you do, and
you that have set before you a high standard of what a
Christian should be, do you not find that before the
breakfast things are cleared away from the table that
you have displayed enough sin to make you ashamed
of yourselves? If we were to shut ourselves up in the
lone cell of a hermit, temptation would follow us; for
as long as we cannot escape from ourselves we cannot
escape from incitements to sin. There is that within
our hearts which should make us watchful and humble before God. If He does not confirm us, we are so
weak that we shall stumble and fall, not overturned by
an enemy but by our own carelessness. Lord, be thou
our strength. We are weakness itself.

Besides that, there is the weariness which comes of
a long life. When we begin our Christian profession
we mount up with wings as eagles. Further on we run
without weariness; but in our best and truest days, we
walk without fainting. Our pace seems slower, but it is
more serviceable and better sustained. I pray God that
the energy of our youth may continue with us as long as
it is the energy of the Spirit and not the mere fermen-
tation of proud flesh. He that has been on the road to
heaven for a long time finds that there was good reason why it was promised that his shoes would be iron
and brass, for the road is rough. He has discovered that
there are Hills of Difficulty and Valleys of Humiliation;
that there is a Vale of Deathshade, and, worse still, a
Vanity Fair—and all these are to be traversed. If there
be Delectable Mountains (and, thank God, there are),

there are also Castles of Despair, the inside of which pilgrims have too often seen. Considering all things, those who hold out to the end in the way of holiness will be "men wondered at" (Zec 3:8).

"O world of wonders, I can say no less." The days of a Christian's life are like so many Kohinoors* of mercy threaded upon the golden string of divine faithfulness. In heaven we shall tell angels and principalities and powers the unsearchable riches of Christ which were spent upon us and enjoyed by us while we were here below. We have been kept alive on the brink of death. Our spiritual life has been a flame burning on in the midst of the sea, a stone that has remained suspended in the air. It will amaze the universe to see us enter the pearly gate, blameless in the day of our Lord Jesus Christ. We should be full of grateful wonder if kept for an hour, and I trust we are.

If this were all, there would be enough cause for anxiety, but there is far more. We have to think of what a place we live in. The world is a howling wilderness to many of God's people. Some of us are greatly indulged in the providence of God, but others have a stern fight of it. We begin our day with prayer, and we hear the voice of holy song very often in our houses; but many good people have scarcely risen from their knees in the mornnig before they are saluted with blasphemy. They go out to work, and all day long they are vexed with filthy conversation like righteous Lot in Sodom. Can you even walk the open streets without your ears being afflicted with foul language?

*The Kohinoor is an Indian diamond, weighing 106 carats; it is now part of the British crown jewels.

The world is no friend to grace. The best we can do with this world is to get through it as quickly as we can, for we dwell in an enemy's country. A robber lurks in every bush. Everywhere we need to travel with a "drawn sword" in our hand, or at least with that weapon which is called "all-prayer" ever at our side, for we have to contend for every inch of our way. Make no mistake about this or you will be rudely shaken out of your fond delusion. O God, help us and confirm us to the end, or where shall we be?

True religion is supernatural at its beginning, supernatural in its continuance, and supernatural in its close. It is the work of God from first to last. There is great need that the hand of the Lord should be stretched out still; that need you are feeling now, and I am glad that you should feel it; for now you will look for your own preservation to the Lord who alone is able to keep us from falling and glorify us with His Son.

18

Confirmation

NOTICE THE SECURITY which Paul confidently expected for all the saints. He says, "Who shall also confirm you unto the end, that ye may be blameless in the day of our Lord Jesus Christ" (1 Co 1:8). This is the kind of confirmation which is to be desired above all things. It supposes that the persons are right, and it proposes to confirm them in the right. It would be an awful thing to confirm a man in ways of sin and error. Think of a confirmed drunkard or a confirmed thief or a confirmed liar. It would be a deplorable thing for a man to be confirmed in unbelief and ungodliness. Divine confirmation can only be enjoyed by those to whom the grace of God has been already manifested. It is the work of the Holy Spirit. He who gives faith strengthens and establishes it; He who kindles love in us preserves it and increases its flame. What He makes us to know by His first teaching, the Holy Spirit causes us to know with greater clearness and certainty by still further instruction. Holy acts are confirmed till they become habits, and holy feelings are confirmed till they become abiding conditions. Experience and practice confirm our beliefs, and our resolutions. Both our joys and our sorrows, our successes and our failures, are sanctified to the selfsame end, even as the tree is helped to take root both by the soft showers and the rough winds. The mind is instructed, and in its growing knowledge it gathers reasons for persevering in the good way. The heart is comforted, and so it is made to cling more closely to the consoling truth. The grip grows tighter, the tread grows firmer, and the man himself becomes more solid and substantial.

This is not a merely natural growth but is as distinct a work of the Spirit as conversion. The Lord will surely give it to those who are relying upon Him for eternal life. By His inward working He will deliver us from being "unstable as water" and cause us to be rooted and grounded. This building us up into Christ Jesus and causing us to abide in Him is a part of the method by which He saves us. You may daily look for this, and you shall not be disappointed. He whom you trust will make you to be as a tree planted by the rivers of waters, so preserved that even your leaf shall not wither.

What a strength to a church is a confirmed Christian! He is a comfort to the sorrowful and a help to the weak. Would you not like to be such? Confirmed believers are pillars in the house of our God. These are not carried away by every wind of doctrine nor overthrown by sudden temptation. They are a great stay to others and act as anchors in the time of church trouble. You who are beginning the holy life hardly dare to hope that you will become like them. But you need not fear; the good Lord will work in you as well as in them. One of these days you who are now a "babe" in Christ shall be a "father" in the Church. Hope for this great thing, but hope for it as a gift of grace and not as the wages of work or as the product of your own energy.

The inspired apostle Paul speaks of these people as to be confirmed unto the end. He expected the grace of God to preserve them personally to the end of their lives, or till the Lord Jesus should come. Indeed, he expected that the whole Church of God in every place and in all time would be kept to the end of the dispensation, till the Lord Jesus as the Bridegroom would come to celebrate the wedding feast with His perfected Bride. All who are in Christ will be confirmed in Him till that illustrious day. Has He not said, "Because I live, ye shall live also" (Jn 14:19)? He also said, "I give unto them [my sheep] eternal life; and they shall never perish, neither shall any man pluck them out of my hand" (Jn 10:28). "He which hath begun a good work in you will perform it until the day of Jesus Christ" (Phil 1:6). The work of grace in the soul is not a superficial reformation; the life implanted as the new birth comes of a living and incorruptible seed which liveth and abideth forever. And the promises of God made to believers are not of a transient character, but involve for their fulfillment the believer's holding on his way till he comes to endless glory. We are "kept by the power of God through faith unto salvation" (1 Pe 1:5). "The righteous also shall hold on his way" (Job 17:9). Not as the result of our own merit or strength, but as a gift of free and undeserved favor those who believe are "preserved in Christ Jesus" (Jude 1). Of the sheep of His fold Jesus will lose none; no member of His Body shall die; no gem of His treasure shall be missing in the day when He makes up His

jewels. The salvation which is received by faith is not
a thing of months and years, for our Lord Jesus hath
"obtained eternal redemption for us" (Heb 9:12), and
that which is eternal cannot come to an end.

Paul also declares his expectation that the Corinthian saints would be confirmed to the end blameless.
(See 1 Co 1:8). This blamelessness is a precious part
of our keeping. To be kept holy is better than merely
to be kept safe. It is a dreadful thing when you see
religious people blundering out of one dishonor into
another; they have not believed in the power of our
Lord to make them blameless. The lives of some pro-
fessing Christians are a series of stumbles; they are
never quite down, and yet they are seldom on their
feet. This is not a fit thing for a believer. He is invited
to walk with God; by faith he can attain steady perseverance in holiness, and he should do so. The Lord
is able, not only to save us from hell, but to keep us
from falling. We need not yield to temptation. Is it
not written, "Sin shall not have dominion over you"
(Ro 6:14)? The Lord is able to keep the feet of His
saints, and He will do it if we will trust Him to do so.
We need not defile our garments; we may by His grace
keep them unspotted from the world. We are bound
to do this, for without holiness "no man shall see the
Lord" (Heb 12:14).

The apostle prophesied for these believers that which
he would have us seek after—that we may be preserved
"blameless in the day of our Lord Jesus Christ" (1 Co
1:8). The American Standard Version has "unreprove-
able" instead of "blameless." Possibly a better render-
ing would be "unimpeachable." God grant that in that

last great day we may stand free from all charge, that none in the whole universe may dare to challenge our claim to be the redeemed of the Lord. We have sins and infirmities to mourn over, but these are not the kind of faults which would prove us to be out of Christ. We shall be clear of hypocrisy, deceit, hatred, and delight in sin, for these things would be fatal charges.

Despite our failings, the Holy Spirit can work in us a character spotless before men so that, like Daniel, we shall furnish no occasion for accusing tongues, except in the matter of our religion. Multitudes of godly men and women have exhibited lives so transparent, so consistent throughout, that none could say anything against them. The Lord will be able to say of many a believer, as he did of Job when Satan stood before Him, "Hast thou considered my servant, . . . a perfect and an upright man, one that feareth God, and escheweth evil?" (1:8). This is what you must look for at the Lord's hands. This is the triumph of the saints, to continue to follow the Lamb wherever He goes, maintaining our integrity as before the living God. May we never turn aside into crooked ways and give cause to the adversary to blaspheme. Of the true believer it is written, "He . . . keepeth himself and that wicked one toucheth him not" (1 Jn 5:18). May it be so written concerning us!

If you are just beginning in the divine life, the Lord can give you an irreproachable character. Even though in your past life you may have gone far into sin, the Lord can altogether deliver you from the power of former habits and make you an example of virtue. Not only can He make you moral, but He can make you abhor every false way and follow after all that is saintly. Do not doubt it. The chief of sinners need not be a step behind the purest of the saints. Believe this, and according to your faith shall it be unto you.

Oh, what a joy it will be to be found blameless in the day of judgment! We sing not amiss when we join in that charming hymn:

> Bold shall I stand in that great day,
> For who aught to my charge shall lay?
> While by my Lord absolved I am,
> From sin's tremendous curse and blame.
>
> ZINZENDORF

What bliss it will be to enjoy that dauntless courage when heaven and earth shall flee away from the face of the Judge of all! This bliss shall be the portion of everyone who looks alone to the grace of God in Christ Jesus and in that sacred might wages continual war with all sin.

19

Why Saints Persevere

THE HOPE which filled the heart of Paul concerning the Corinthian brethren we have already seen to be full of comfort to those who trembled as to their future. But why was it that he believed that the brethren would be confirmed unto the end?

I want you to notice that he gives his reasons. Here they are: "God is faithful, by whom ye were called unto the fellowship of his Son Jesus Christ" (1 Co 1:9).

The apostle does not say, "*You* are faithful." The faithfulness of man is very unreliable; it is mere vanity. He does not say, "You have faithful ministers to lead and guide you, and therefore I trust you will be safe." Oh, no! If we are kept by men we shall be badly kept. He says, "God is faithful." If we are found faithful, it will be because God is faithful. On the faithfulness of our covenant God the whole burden of our salvation must rest. On this glorious attribute of God the matter hinges. We are variable as the wind, frail as a spider's web, weak as water. No dependence can be placed upon our natural qualities or our spiritual attainments, but God abideth faithful. He is faithful in His love; He knows no variableness, neither shadow of turning.

He is faithful to His purpose; He does not begin a work and then leave it undone. He is faithful to His relationships. As a Father He will not renounce His children, as a Friend He will not deny His people, as a Creator He will not forsake the work of His own hands. He is faithful to His promises and will never allow one of them to fail for a single believer. He is faithful to His covenant, which He has made with us in Christ Jesus and ratified with the blood of His sacrifice. He is faithful to His Son and will not allow His precious blood to be spilled in vain. He is faithful to His people to whom He has promised eternal life and from whom He will not turn away.

This faithfulness of God is the foundation and cornerstone of our hope of final perseverance. The saints shall persevere in holiness because God perseveres in grace. He perseveres to bless, and therefore believers persevere in being blessed. He continues to keep His people, and therefore they continue to keep His commandments. This is good solid ground to rest upon, and it is delightfully consistent with the title of this book, *All of Grace*. Thus it is free favor and infinite mercy which ring in the dawn of salvation, and the same sweet bells sound melodiously through the whole day of grace.

You see that the only reasons for hoping that we shall be confirmed to the end and be found blameless at the last are found in our God, but in Him these reasons are exceedingly abundant.

They lie first in what God has done. He has gone so far in blessing us that it is not possible for Him to run back. Paul reminds us that He has called us "unto the fellowship of his Son Jesus Christ" (1 Co 1:9). Has He called us? Then the call cannot be reversed, for "the gifts and calling of God are without repentance" (Ro 11:29). From the effectual call of His grace the Lord never turns. "Whom he called, them he also justified: and whom he justified, them he also glorified" (Ro 8:30); this is the invariable rule of the divine procedure. There is a common call of which it is said, "Many are called, but few are chosen" (Mt 22:14), but this of which we are now thinking is another kind of call which means special love and necessitates the possession of that to which we are called. In such a case it is with the called one even as with Abraham's seed, of whom the Lord said, "Thou whom I have taken from the ends of the earth, and called thee from the chief men thereof, and said unto thee, Thou art my servant; I have chosen thee, and not cast thee away" (Is 41:9).

In what the Lord has done, we see strong reasons for our preservation and future glory because the Lord has called us into the fellowship of His Son Jesus Christ. It means into partnership with Jesus Christ, and I would have you carefully consider what this means. If you are indeed called by divine grace, you have come into fellowship with the Lord Jesus Christ, and are joint-owner with Him in all things. Henceforth you are one with Him in the sight of the Most High. The Lord Jesus bare your sins in His own body on the tree, being made a curse for you, and at the same time He has become your righteousness so that you are justified in Him. You are Christ's and Christ is yours. As Adam stood for his descendants, so does Jesus stand for all who are in Him. As husband and wife are one,

so is Jesus one with all those who are united to Him
by faith; one by a conjugal union which can never be
broken. More than this, believers are members of the
Body of Christ and so they are one with Him by a
loving, living, lasting union. God has called us into
this union, this fellowship, this partnership, and by this
very fact He has given us the token and pledge of our
being confirmed to the end. If we were considered
apart from Christ, we would be poor perishable units,
soon dissolved and borne away to destruction; but as
one with Jesus we are made partakers of His nature
and are endowed with His immortal life. Our destiny
is linked with that of our Lord, and until *He* can be
destroyed it is not possible that we would perish.

Dwell much upon this partnership with the Son of
God, unto which you have been called, for all your
hope lies there. You can never be poor while Jesus is
rich because you are in one firm with Him. Want can
never assail you, since you are joint-proprietor with
Him who is Possessor of heaven and earth. You can
never fail, for though one of the partners in the firm is
as poor as a church mouse and in himself an utter
bankrupt who could not pay even a small amount of
his heavy debts, yet the other Partner is inconceivably,
inexhaustibly rich. In such a partnership you are raised
above the depression of the times, the changes of the
future, and the shock of the end of all things. The
Lord has called you into the fellowship of His Son
Jesus Christ, and by that act and deed He has put you
into the place of infallible safeguard.

If you are indeed a believer, you are one with Jesus,
and therefore you are secure. Do you not see that it

must be so? You must be confirmed to the end until the day of His appearing, if you have indeed been made one with Jesus by the irrevocable act of God. Christ and the believing sinner are in the same boat; unless Jesus sinks, the believer will never drown. Jesus has taken His redeemed into such connection with Himself that He must first be smitten, overcome, and dishonored before the least of His purchased ones can be injured. His name is at the head of the firm, and until it can be dishonored we are secure against all dread of failure.

So, then, with the utmost confidence let us go forward into the unknown future, linked eternally with Jesus. If the men of the world should cry, "Who is this that cometh up from the wilderness, leaning upon her beloved?" (Song 8:5) we will joyfully confess that we do lean on Jesus and that we mean to lean on Him more and more. Our faithful God is an ever-flowing well of delight, and our fellowship with the Son of God is a full river of joy. Knowing these glorious things, we cannot be discouraged. No, rather we cry with the apostle, "Who shall separate us from the love of . . . God, which is in Christ Jesus our Lord?" (Ro 8:35-39).

20

Conclusion

IF YOU HAVE not followed me step by step as you have
read these pages, I am truly sorry. Book reading is of
small value unless the truths which pass before the
mind are grasped, appropriated, and carried out in a
practical way. It is as if one saw plenty of food in a
store and yet remained hungry for want of personally
eating some. It is all in vain that you and I have met
unless you have actually laid hold upon Christ Jesus
my Lord. On my part there was a distinct desire to
benefit you, and I have done my best to that end. It
pains me that I have not been able to do you good, for
I have longed to win that privilege. I was thinking of
you when I wrote this page, and I laid down my pen
and solemnly bowed in prayer for everyone who would
read it. It is my firm conviction that great numbers of
readers will get a blessing, even though *you* refuse to
be of the number. But why should *you* refuse? If you
do not desire the choice blessing which I would have
brought to you, at least do me the justice to admit
that the blame of your final doom will not lie at my
door. When we meet before the great white throne
you will not be able to charge me with having idly

used the attention which you were pleased to give me while you were reading my book. God knows I wrote each line for your eternal good. I now in spirit take you by the hand with a firm grip. Do you feel my brotherly grasp? The tears are in my eyes as I look at you and say, *Why will you die?* Will you not give your soul a thought? Will you perish through sheer carelessness? Oh, do not do so, but weigh these solemn matters and make sure of eternity! Do not refuse Jesus, His love, His blood, His salvation. Why should you do so? Can you do it? *I beseech you, do not turn away from your Redeemer!*

If, on the other hand, my prayers are heard and you have been led to trust the Lord Jesus and receive from Him salvation by grace, then keep this doctrine and this way of living. Let Jesus be your all in all, and let free grace be the one line in which you live and move. There is no life like that of one who lives in the favor of God. To receive all as a free gift preserves the mind from self-righteous pride and from self-accusing despair. It makes the heart grow warm with grateful love, and thus it creates a feeling in the soul which is infinitely more acceptable to God than anything that can possibly come of slavish fear. Those who hope to be saved by trying to do their best know nothing of that glowing fervor, that hallowed warmth, that devout joy in God which come with salvation freely given according to the grace of God. The slavish spirit of self-salvation is no match for the joyous spirit of adoption. There is more real virtue in the least emotion of faith than in all the efforts of legal bondslaves or all the weary machinery of devotees who would climb to heaven by

fantasies about making love paled in comparison to reality.

He touched the sensitive top of her femininity. ''Oh, Dawson—''

''What, sweetheart? Do you want me to stop? If you do,'' he said, his voice raspy, his chest heaving, ''speak now or forever hold your peace. I'm gettin' awfully close to the point of no return—''

''No,'' she gasped. ''Don't you dare stop.''

It felt too wonderful for words. When he slid his finger inside her, the pulsating increased. She needed to know the final mystery of mating. She wanted him inside her.

She slid her hand down to his waist, and a groan escaped him. His response nurtured her female soul, and she reveled in her power to turn him on. She started to move her hand lower, then stopped, suddenly shy. He took her fingers and rested them over him. The soft thickness felt right in her hand, like velvet over steel. She stroked him until he groaned.

Suddenly and in one fluid motion, he rolled her to her back, then levered himself on top of her. Spreading her legs wider with his knee, he positioned himself against her. She felt a hard probing at the intimate entrance to her body. She gasped, feeling anticipation as well as a little trepidation. Then he gently pushed.

She felt his passion, his desire, his confusion as he encountered her tightness.

''Mattie, what—'' He went still. ''Are you—''

Every cell, nerve and muscle in her body screamed out in protest. She had waited for this too long. She was more than ready. He was half a heartbeat from pulling away. No way was he backing out now.

Mattie raised her hips to meet his thrust, and felt

his entry followed by a swift tearing pain. She gasped at the sharp discomfort and buried her face in his neck. His arms came around her and just held her until, in a matter of moments, the ache diminished. She sensed his tension and need for release, even as she felt his restraint in the bulging muscles of his arms. But she didn't want restraint. She wanted to experience it all.

"It's all right," she whispered. She wrapped her legs around his waist, drawing him deeper inside her. "I want to know everything."

He moaned, and she could almost feel his surrender. Then he drove into her. His breathing was a rough rasp in her ear, but the movement produced delicious sensations that made her heart race and her blood sing. She quickly learned the rhythm and moved with him. His urgency was contagious, fueling her own rising passion. The feelings were more powerful, more profound than she'd ever imagined. With Dawson, she rose higher and higher until bright light consumed her. Her world shattered into a thousand shards of glass.

As she drifted back to earth on a golden cloud, delicious aftershocks rippled through her. At the same time, Dawson strained, and she watched his face, the concentration in his features, the tension in his jaw. Then he lunged once more and stopped, groaning as he found release. Now that she knew the wondrous feeling herself, she was very happy to give to him in return.

Completely spent, Dawson lowered himself against her, then rolled to his back. He was still breathing hard. In the moonlight, she saw the astonishment mixed with anger on his face. She didn't understand. For several moments she watched him as he dragged air into his lungs.

"What's wrong?" she asked, pulling the sheet up over them.

"Why didn't you tell me you're a virgin?"

"I'm not."

"Don't be cute, Mattie. This isn't the time for cute. I suspected, but you told me about the jerk—when you were sixteen. I wasn't sure."

"I was merely calling a spade a spade. I am not a virgin."

"But you were until a couple of minutes ago."

She grinned. "What a wonderful thing. The world's oldest living virgin is now...not."

"This is serious," he snapped.

"I don't see why. We're both over twenty-one."

"One of us just barely," he said. There was self-loathing in his tone.

She ignored his comment and went on. "I'm an adult. I know my own mind. What's your problem?"

"For starters, I would have done it differently."

"Then I'm glad I didn't say anything, because I thought it was perfect." She turned to her side to look at him. "But for argument's sake, what would you have done differently?"

"Not that you deserve a response, but I would have gone more slowly. I would have taken the time to get you ready."

"I was ready. You don't get it, do you? I've been ready for years. Don't beat yourself up over it, Dawson." She frowned. "But I'm being selfish. Maybe *you* needed more time to get ready."

"Mattie, this is serious to me. Taking a woman's virginity is a responsibility. I guess I just wasn't prepared for exactly how inexperienced you are."

"I don't see what my experience or lack thereof has to do with anything. Sooner or later it has to go."

"Right. To the man you marry. Now—"

"What are you saying, Dawson?"

Just then Mattie heard the hall door to the bedroom next door open. The light went on in the bathroom, and she heard a soft knock.

"Mattie, you awake? I heard you talking."

Griff!

Before she could even sit up, the door swung open and her brother stood there backlit by the bathroom light. She was grateful that she couldn't see his expression.

When he charged the bed, Mattie was glad that she was closest to him.

Griff loomed over her, but he glared at Dawson. "We had a deal. I told you to watch over my sister, not sleep with her yourself."

"Hold on, Griff. This doesn't concern you," Dawson said.

Deal? Mattie went cold.

"The hell it doesn't concern me. Is this how you fulfill your responsibilities? When the cat's away…"

It was happening all over again, Mattie thought. It didn't matter that she was grown-up now. All the humiliation and pain she'd felt as a kid flooded her. She glanced at Dawson, who was watching her brother.

Griff glared at them for several moments, then said, "I plan to break you in two, Prescott."

Mattie already felt broken in two. Dawson was watching over her at Griff's command? That explained a lot, like why he'd been underfoot. And why he'd taken her to dinner. But the pain and betrayal were grinding through her. It was just like the last time. She had feelings for a guy. She acted on them. She got kicked in the teeth.

"You've got one minute, Prescott," Griff said, then turned on his heel and disappeared through the connecting bathroom.

Dawson pulled on briefs and slacks in about ten seconds flat, and followed, leaving Mattie alone in the bed. Anger closed in on her. He had only paid attention to her because Griff had intimidated him into the job. In essence, he'd hired a baby-sitter. She'd thought nothing could be worse than her humbling teenage experience. But this beat it by a mile. And she knew why.

She actually cared for Dawson.

If she hadn't, she wouldn't have slept with him. After sharing the intimacy, she now knew there was no way she could have done something so personal and private with just anyone.

It hurt deeply to know that Dawson had no feelings for her. To him it was probably nothing more than guard duty. Undercover work, so to speak. But the double entendre held no humor for her. After her makeover, when the cowboys had begun to take an interest in her, he must have stepped up surveillance, she realized. Making love had just been an assignment to him.

Her eyes burned with tears she wanted badly to let fall. But she wouldn't give him the satisfaction. She heard angry voices from the other room. She almost wished Griff would pop Dawson one. But no. Her brother was really furious. Dawson might actually get hurt.

Humiliated as she was, Mattie had no intention of being left out of this. Griff had no right to do anything.

He was out of bounds involving Dawson as body-guard, and he had no business meting out punishment according to his own macho perception of right and wrong.

She threw the sheet back and jumped out of bed. After pulling on jeans and a shirt, she hurried through the connecting bath as the sound of male voices rose.

She walked into Griff's room, which was almost a duplicate of her own—double bed, distressed-wood dresser and nightstands, chair ottoman and table lamp in the corner and Western prints on the walls. Griff and Dawson stood at the foot of the bed. They were practically nose to nose, and were scowling at each other.

"This is all my fault," Dawson was saying. "Mattie's not to blame."

Anger pushed aside the pain she felt over his betrayal. "Why does anyone have to be blamed?" she asked. "We're consenting adults."

Neither man looked at her.

"I ought to tear you limb from limb," Griff ground out.

"Go ahead. It's no less than I deserve. But don't expect me to make it easy for you."

Mattie put her hands on her hips. "There will be no limb tearing."

They both ignored her.

"Dawson, what the hell were you thinking?" Griff poked his chest. "I guess the real question is which body part were you thinking *with?*"

Dawson smacked his hand away. "I take full responsibility for what happened."

Griff lifted his fists. "Damn right you'll take responsibility. I believe in justice, swift and sure."

"If you think it will solve something, I'm ready."
Dawson widened his stance and bent his knees
slightly.

That does it, Mattie thought.

She moved forward and insinuated herself between
the two men. Size was on their side so she needed
leverage. She rammed her shoulder into Griff and hit
him somewhere in the chest area. He grunted as the
wind was knocked out of him from the surprise attack.
While she had him off balance, she put all her weight
behind the move and drove him backwards a foot or
so. When he regained his balance, he grabbed her
shoulders. "Mattie, what the heck is wrong with
you?"

"I'm getting sick and tired of people carrying on
conversations about me right in front of me. As if I
wasn't even here," she added for good measure. Her
chest rose and fell rapidly from the force of her emotions and the effort of moving a man the size of her
brother.

"I'll handle this, Mattie," Dawson said, putting his
hands on her arms and gently moving her to the side,
out of the way.

She rounded on him, glaring. Venting her rage felt
wonderful. "Who do you think you are? You're a two-
bit, low-down, underhanded, lying, scheming stuffed
shirt!"

She looked at his bare chest and realized how wrong
she was. He wasn't even *wearing* a shirt. It made her
mad that she could notice the coarse dark hair across
his muscular, masculine chest. She was madder
still that he could affect her at all after what she'd
found out.

"Mattie, calm down," he said. "I'm going to do the honorable thing."

"Damn right, you are," Griff growled. He moved to stand beside Dawson.

"I don't know what you're talking about, and I don't much care," she said. "Dawson and I did nothing wrong, Griff. You have no right to come in here like this. Like a—a Cro-Magnon man."

Griff still looked angry. "Mattie, I'm your brother. I love you, and it's my job to look out for you."

"Says who?"

"No one. But Reed is on his honeymoon and Brody is about to get married. That leaves me to take over. It's just understood."

"Well, I don't understand," she said. "And I've had enough. You've been butting into my love life ever since Frank Sinclair."

"Who's he?" Dawson asked with unmistakable menace in his voice.

Griff glanced at him. "He worked on the ranch when she was a kid. She had a crush on him. She told him how she felt, and he came to us. We made sure no one got close again." He glared at Dawson. "'Til now."

There was so much more that couldn't even be put into words. But thanks to the brothers Fortune, no man had gotten close since that day.

And no man had been able to take the sting out of the experience. Until now, she thought, echoing Griff's words as she looked at Dawson. She saw the pity in his eyes, and hated it.

"As mad as I am at you, Griffin Fortune, I do appreciate the fact that you care about me. But I will handle this."

"How?"

"What kind of a question is that?" she asked. "Just forget about it. What else is there to do?"

"Not damn likely we'll pretend it didn't happen," Griff said, meeting Dawson's look.

When the two men nodded slightly, Mattie wondered if there was some unspoken testosterone-fueled method of communication that only men understood.

"What do you mean?" she asked.

"You're going to marry him," Griff declared, just as Dawson said, "I'm going to marry you."

Nine

"Marry me? I've just discovered that you're the lying, cheating spawn of the devil—and you want to *marry* me?"

Dawson winced as the pitch in Mattie's voice escalated to a level that only he and dogs could hear. Not to mention the words *spawn of the devil*. How many times had he told himself he would never sink to the same level as his father? Before he could give that any more thought, she started to laugh. But there was a tinge of hysteria mixed in.

"I get it," she said, wiping her eyes. "Dawson, you're too much. Your first practical joke worked so well, you decided to try another one."

"What joke?" he asked.

"The one where you pretended to be interested in me while you were in cahoots with my brother to keep me from having any fun."

He met her gaze and willed her to understand. "Mattie, let's get one thing straight, here and now. I never pretend."

Especially about what had transpired between them tonight. He couldn't say for sure about her, but taking Mattie to bed had been the best thing he could remember in longer than he wanted to think about. Common sense told him that saying so in front of her brother would be a big mistake. He would lay money on the fact that Griff was mentally scrolling through his repertoire of three hundred ways to kill a man with his bare hands as he calculated the merits of each—as in, which one would hurt the most for the second-and-a-half it took Dawson to die.

Griff wasn't someone he wanted to make an enemy of. Which made him grateful that they were on the same wavelength. They both agreed on the issue of changing Mattie's marital status based on Dawson's participation in tonight's events.

She shook her head. "Maybe your term for it is 'play acting.' Whatever you want to call it, the fact is, it worked. Really well. But I guarantee you'll never sucker me again."

"It was no joke, Mattie. Not to me. In fact, I started to tell you what was going on, but you sidetracked me. And the bottom line is that now none of that matters. I want you to marry me."

"Why?" she asked.

"Because it's the right thing to do."

He winced for the second time in as many minutes. But this time it was because his words extinguished the light of expectation and hope in her eyes.

"Damn straight, it's right," Griff said. "And the sooner, the better." Obviously agitated, he ran a hand through his hair. "Since there's already a wedding in progress, maybe Brody and Jillian wouldn't mind making it a double—"

"Griff!" Mattie cried, glaring at him as if he were a wrestler asking to join a royal tea party. "This isn't a drink, and they aren't bartenders. Even if I wanted to—which I don't—I can't just walk up to Jillian and Brody and say 'make it a double.'"

Dawson wasn't so sure. He thought Griff's idea had

some value. Preparations were definitely going on. People were already planning to attend. The guest lists would be almost identical. Because of Jillian's pregnancy, she and Brody had decided to keep it small— mostly family and very close friends. Just a couple of days away, the date wouldn't give Mattie a chance to think this to death and then back out.

Once he convinced her to go along in the first place, of course.

Unfortunately, his mother was away and there wouldn't be time to get her here. But he would make it up to her. For as long as he could remember, he'd been making it up to her for the fact that his father had used her, then turned his back when he wanted a younger woman. And that's exactly the reason he was determined to marry Mattie. No one would ever have to make up to her for anything he had done. Unlike his father, Dawson would take responsibility for his actions. Period.

"A double wedding." Dawson nodded thoughtfully as he looked at the other man. "You may be on to something, Griff. I'll talk to Brody and see what he thinks. He and Jillian will be here in the morning for breakfast and a progress report on preparations for their wedding, anyway."

Griff nodded approval. "Good idea."

Mattie shook her head. "You guys are doing it again—talking as if I'm not here." She took her brother by the shirt front and pulled him down so they were nose to nose. "Read my lips. I'm not marrying Dawson or anyone else."

"Why not?" he asked. "I thought you wanted to get married and have a baby. Soon. Seems like it would be a good idea to make it legal." His eyes darkened and he never raised his voice, but there was no mistaking the threat there. "Since you already got a jump start on the baby part."

Good Lord, Dawson thought, he hadn't even considered *that* possibility. He had never been that irresponsible about birth control. But somehow where Mattie Fortune was concerned, all the rules went out the window, right along with his self-control.

But Griff was right. What if there was a baby? Even if there wasn't, Dawson had taken Mattie's virginity. Conscience and his personal code of honor dictated that he make an honest woman of her. He realized, though, that if he phrased it that way to her, he would need to duck and run.

"He's right, Mattie," Dawson said, taking the coward's way out and letting Griff's phrasing stand. "Like I said before, it's the right thing to do."

"For who? You keep saying it's right, but this is *not* the way my fantasy went."

"What fantasy?" Dawson asked.

She turned to him. "Ever since I was a little girl, I've dreamed of how it would be. Me. The man I love. A candlelight dinner. A proposal on bended knee accompanied by a declaration of undying love. When I pictured it, not even one of my brothers was there to spoil the moment. Siblings on deck sort of ruin the romance, if you know what I mean. This isn't even close to my daydream." Misery and betrayal brimmed in her eyes. She waved her hand dismissively. "Oh, look who I'm trying to reason with—Ugg and friend, the caveman conspiracy. I won't do it. You can't force me. Count me out. End of conversation," she said, and stalked back into her room.

Dawson went after her. Griff was right behind him.

Before Dawson could say anything, her brother started in. "You can't run away from this, Mattie."

"Says who?" She grabbed her denim jacket off the chair. "Watch me."

Griff took her arm in a gentle grip, but she couldn't break his hold without a struggle and probably not even then. "Not so fast," he said. "You're not going anywhere. Besides, I've got a question for you."

"Oh, yeah? What?"

"When I left Texas you were hardly more than a girl. Now you look like a woman. Who are you and what have you done with my little sister?" His tone was quiet and gruff, but unmistakably affectionate.

Dawson remembered asking her the same thing after her transformation. It occurred to him that her brother was seeing her for the first time since she'd changed her look *and* lost her virginity. It was a lot to absorb, and Dawson knew that if this were about his own sister, he would probably behave the same way as Griff.

Not to mention that buttering her up with flattery was a stroke of genius. For a secret-agent guy, Griff was okay in the diplomacy department. The question was, would it work?

Dawson was encouraged by the gradual, grudging softening in Mattie's expression.

"What do you mean?" she asked Griff.

"Your hair..." He shrugged, his gaze taking her in from head to toe. "I don't know. You just look different."

"Good or bad different?" There was skepticism in her tone.

"Good." He studied her, then nodded emphatically. "Definitely good different."

"Thank you." She reached both arms out and gave

him a big hug. "And I was very worried about you. I'm awfully glad that you're home safe and sound." She lowered her arms and stepped back. "Nice try, Griff. But it's not going to work. I still won't marry Dawson."

"Why the hell not?" Griff jammed his hands on his hips. "He slept with you, and he's willing to do the manly thing and marry you."

"I slept with him, too. I'm doing the womanly thing and saying no. I have that right because I take just as much responsibility as he does. And I'm exercising my female prerogative to turn him down. Flat," she said, glaring first at her brother, then at Dawson.

Dawson scratched his head. Strike one for diplomacy. It was time for honesty. He looked at her brother. "Griff, could you give us a couple of minutes alone?"

"Why?" The other man looked like he would rather wrestle a five-hundred-pound alligator than leave any man alone with his little sister.

But at this point, it was sort of like closing the barn door after the horses got out. Judging by the scowl on the other man's face, Dawson decided, he'd better not point that out.

"I'd like to talk to her privately," he said. "This is something that concerns the two of us and I think we need some time to discuss where we go from here."

Glancing from Dawson to Mattie, Griff finally said warily, "Okay, but I'll be in the other room. Don't try to slip out the back, Prescott."

"The thought never entered my mind."

"If you need me, Mattie—"

"I won't," she interrupted.

After the doors between the two rooms were closed, Dawson said, "I understand why you're upset—"

"No, you don't," she said, shaking her head. "You don't have a clue what it feels like to be set up, then have the props knocked out from under you."

"Okay. Let's table the patronizing. I'll skip to the groveling part. I apologize for deceiving you, Mattie."

She sniffed. "From grovel to glib in the blink of an eye. You're good, Dawson."

He hadn't expected this to be easy, but she was really being stubborn. Probably because she'd been hurt before. Again, he wanted five minutes alone with the jerk who'd done this to her.

Knowing anger was unproductive, he tamped it down, making way for the guilt. Someone had hurt her, yet she'd given him a chance. And he'd betrayed her trust. Maybe if he tried to explain…

"Griff thought it was best that you didn't know he'd asked me to keep an eye on you. I agreed—reluctantly." He took in a deep breath. "In fact, I started to tell you tonight, before we—"

"Yeah," she said. Her cheeks turned pink with embarrassment. "I know what we did." Her voice was filled with self-recrimination.

That wasn't his intent. He would never want her to regret an experience that he'd found more satisfying—more wonderful—than anything he'd experienced in a long time. And he wasn't even sure why it had blown him away. Certainly not because she was accomplished at it, he thought wryly. But maybe that was her charm: the fact that it was her first time. Her innocence captivated him, along with the earthiness around the edges that was so appealing. Her zest for life was genuine and profoundly seductive.

The only thing he regretted was putting her in this position. Her brothers had kept her pure for the man she would marry. Now he would be that man.

He shook his head, trying to clear away the mental image of pure Mattie without a stitch of clothing, soft and sweet in his arms. He watched her, watching him as if she didn't believe a word that came out of his mouth. He would prove to her that he always meant what he said.

He rammed his fingers through his hair. "Although you probably won't believe this, I really was going to confess."

"Yeah, and next week I'm playing the harp for the San Antonio philharmonic."

"Sarcasm doesn't suit you, Matilda," he said.

She pointed at him. "I told you never to call me that."

"I remember. Because life as I know it would cease to exist. Here's a news flash—it already has."

"Well, there's a lot of that going around."

"I tried to tell you, Mattie. But I seem to remember you putting your hand over my mouth and doing some other things that distracted me." Her eyes widened slightly, and he was pretty sure she remembered the moment, too. "I don't expect you to admit it. The point is, I don't say anything I don't mean. And I mean to marry you. If you want a bended-knee proposal, I don't have a serious objection to that."

"No objection? Well, why didn't you say so before?" She raised one eyebrow. "Be still, my heart. Why do I feel like a potential client you're attempting to dazzle?" She held up her hand. "But let's leave that for a moment. A bended-knee proposal is small potatoes. What about the declaration of undying love?''

He squirmed. That was more complicated. ''Like I said, I won't lie to you. Dishonesty is not my style, even if I didn't care about you. Which I do. If I didn't—care about you, that is—we wouldn't be in this fix in the first place.''

She smiled, her full lips wavery. ''Be still, my heart,'' she said again. But the sardonic look disappeared, opening a small window to her hurt. Her voice softened. ''Somewhere in there I think I might have heard the world's smallest compliment.''

''But love—'' He ran a hand through his hair again and let out a long breath. ''I can tell you without hesitation that I respect you. I care about you. And after what I did, I refuse to walk away from you without making it right.''

''I'm mad as hell that you didn't tell me right away what Griff was up to.''

''You have every right to be,'' he said.

''I thought we tabled patronizing.''

''Sorry,'' he said sheepishly. He would have to learn not to underestimate her.

She tucked a strand of blond hair behind her ear. ''I appreciate the fact that you want to take responsibility. Truly I do. But don't you see, Dawson? I don't want to be anyone's responsibility. This should be the happiest day of my life. And it's not. Only that episode when I was sixteen takes a back seat to this.''

God, he hated topping the first jerk to hurt her. ''I'm sorry, Mattie. If I could change things, I would. But I have to ask, and I want you to really think about this. Will you marry me?''

"Don't think I'm an ungrateful wretch, but my answer has to be no."

Strike two for honesty.

The door opened and Griff stuck his head in. "You two have been talking in here for an awfully long time. What's the verdict, Dawson?"

He gave her brother a thumbs-down. "No go." It was time for reinforcements. "Griff, if you want to take a shot at convincing her, I wouldn't be offended."

"Well, I would," Mattie said. "Don't you guys know how to take no for an answer?" she asked.

"No," they said together.

For good measure, Griff stood in front of the door to his room, cutting off that escape route. Glancing over his shoulder, Dawson gauged the distance to the hall door and took two steps back to position himself so that she couldn't slip around behind him.

Dawson folded his arms over his chest. "Have at it, Griff."

The other man nodded. "Mattie," he began, "your brothers and I consider ourselves open-minded men." He ignored her rude, disbelieving sound and continued, "We understand that this sort of thing—"

"Define 'this sort of thing.'" There was a gleam in her eyes as she watched her brother squirm.

Dawson noted and admired Mattie's tenacious streak. She might be backed into a corner, but she wasn't going down by herself.

"You know. Sex," he mumbled. "It happens all the time with no strings attached."

"Since when are the lot of you understanding about me having sex?" she asked. "You guys have made it your mission in life to keep me pure as the driven snow."

"Until the right guy came along," Griff qualified.

"Or until I slept with one automatically qualifying him as Mr. Right," she shot back, sliding Dawson a look.

"Okay," Griff said, hands on hips as he nodded angrily. "I tried to reason with you, but it's time to get down and dirty."

More reinforcements? Dawson thought.

"What will your Mom and Dad think about this? Have you given that any thought?" Griff asked.

She looked stricken. It was the first chink in her armor that Dawson had ever seen. Some of the spirit seemed to drain out of her, and he hated being responsible for it. Apparently, there were some hurdles that stopped even Mattie Fortune dead in her tracks. He admired her devotion to family, while at the same time despising himself for going along with this to get what he wanted. To salve his own conscience. On his mental spreadsheet, he noted it in the Doing the Wrong Thing for the Right Reason column.

"Griff's right, Mattie. What do you think this will do to your parents?" he asked.

She caught her lower lip between her teeth and worried it as she thought. Finally she said, "They don't have to know."

"Do you really think they won't find out?" Griff asked.

"You wouldn't tell them," she scoffed.

"I will if I have to," her brother threatened. "Even if I didn't, your mother doesn't miss much. Halfway around the world as she is, she'll smell something fishy. She has a radar that would give air traffic controllers a run for their money."

Dawson thought about his own mother. He loved

her, but he couldn't say that she was particularly intuitive about him. Too bad. It might have been nice.

Mattie paced the room like a caged tigress. At one point, Dawson thought she was eyeing the window as an escape route, and he tensed, ready to stop her if need be. But she turned around and faced them both, head held high.

There was anger, hurt and violation in the stormy look she leveled at her brother and then at him. "If it were just to quiet the likes of you two, I would never in a million years agree to this. But you hit below the belt, Griff. Maybe that's why you're so good at whatever it is that you do on your secret trips."

"Mattie, I'm—"

"Stuff a sock in it. When you're right, you're right. Mom *will* know. Damn it."

Dawson didn't blame her for lashing out. This obviously hurt her a lot. The look in her eyes tied his gut in knots. If he could rewind the tape and fix things, he would do it in a flash. Since he couldn't, there was a part of him glad that she was weakening.

"I would rather die than do anything to cause my mother and father pain or worry or embarrassment. All right," she said looking at Dawson. "If the offer's still good, I'll marry you."

"The offer's still good," he said.

"Don't bother going down on one knee. We both know this isn't about me or what I want. It's not about love. It's about your overactive sense of honor. More's the pity," she said sadly.

From the moment he'd met her, Dawson had been trying to treat her as a child. Tonight she'd admitted to having girlish fantasies. But it gave him no satisfaction to discover that. He felt like the muck on the underside of a rock at the bottom of a lake. Not even a river where the garbage washed away. He was stagnant slime.

He'd singlehandedly been responsible for the death of her dream.

After a sleepless night, Mattie met her brother and his fiancé at the front door the following morning. She sent Brody to talk to Dawson and her uncle Ryan in the great room. With little or no coaxing, Mattie took Jillian on a tour of the outer courtyard where wedding preparations were under way. As they surveyed the outer adobe walls surrounding the stone patio, the fragrance of roses drifted to her. She breathed in the perfume, finding a small bit of comfort. This setting was idyllic: a garden filled with purple sage plants, ornamental grasses in shades of green and blue, roses and jasmine.

Mattie thought this a perfect place for her wedding. If Jillian agreed. Now it was time to broach the subject with her soon-to-be sister-in-law. She, Griff and Dawson had agreed to keep the reason behind the hurriedness of the marriage secret.

"I have an announcement to make," she said, nervously twisting her fingers together. Before Jillian could make a comment or even ask what, Mattie blurted out, "Dawson asked me to marry him, and I said yes."

Jillian's jaw dropped. She blinked a couple of times and finally said, "You and Dawson?"

"Yeah, I know it's sudden," Mattie answered, her cheeks burning. "But—"

"You and Dawson?"

"Strange, huh? I'm not sure I understand it myself. It just sort of happened."

"You and Dawson?"

Mattie glared at her. "Will you stop saying that?"

"I need to sit down," Jillian said. She lowered her pregnant fanny into the cushy pad on a wrought-iron chair that had been pushed to the side, making room for reception paraphernalia. She shook her head. "I knew you were up to something when you reinvented yourself."

"I what?"

The other woman waved her hand dismissively. "Oh, it's the politically correct term for getting a makeover. But I never in a million years guessed that you'd set your sights on Dawson Prescott. Or that you and Fortune's financial wizard had gotten so serious, so fast."

Numbers weren't the only thing he was a wizard at, Mattie thought, shivering at remembered pleasures from his gifted hands. How she wished she could tell her friend the truth. That she'd been pressured into this decision and was emotionally blackmailed into the marriage because she and Dawson had slept together. But she decided it was best to keep that detail to herself. She knew Jillian told Brody everything. Somehow it would get back to her mother and father. As soon as she worked up the courage, she would call home and tell them she was getting married. But she would spare them the ugly reality of why she was doing it.

How had the most wonderful night of her life landed her in the biggest mess of her life?

She plastered a sunny smile on her face and felt the ache start in her cheeks. She figured she'd best get used to it, since the next couple of days would be a repeat of what she was going through now. "It was love at first sight."

"Have you set a date?"

"Well, that's what I wanted to talk to you about. Since Dawson's sister and my brother Reed are going to be here for your wedding before going on to live in Australia, I was wondering—"

Jillian clapped her hands. "A double ceremony!"

Mentally, she breathed a sigh of relief that she was spared the asking. "I don't want you to feel you have to say yes."

"Of course not."

"We just thought it might be advantageous—"

"Convenience shouldn't be a consideration when you're talking about love," Jillian scolded good-naturedly.

If they were talking about love, Mattie would have agreed with her. But this whole thing came under the heading of Suffering the Consequences of Your Actions. And *suffering* was the key word.

She just couldn't quite figure out why Dawson was doing it. Griff was intimidating, but the instincts she relied on with her horses told her that her fiancé wasn't afraid of her brother. So what was his reason for going through with this farce of a marriage?

"I think it's a great idea," Jillian said.

"Really? You wouldn't feel as if you're having to share the limelight?"

"I love the idea of sharing the limelight with you."

"You're sure you wouldn't hate me forever?" Mattie met her gaze squarely. "Before you answer, think very carefully."

"I don't have to think carefully. My answer is that

it will be twice as wonderful for Brody and me if you and Dawson join in our happiness.''

Mattie breathed a sigh. ''All right. Then it's settled—''

''I just thought of something. We'll have the same anniversary.''

Mattie's head was spinning from everything she'd thought about. ''That's true.''

''Oh, no,'' Jillian said. ''I just thought of something else. And this is a potential problem.''

After what she'd been through, Mattie couldn't take another problem—potential, implied or real. ''What?'' she asked, tensing.

''You're supposed to be my bridesmaid. How can you be a bride at the same time?''

Breathing a sigh of relief, Mattie shook her head. ''I don't see any problem. We'll just stand up together and take vows one at a time.''

''But your bridesmaid's dress is green velvet for my ceremony. Don't you want to wear traditional white for yours?''

Nothing about this was traditional, Mattie thought as profound sadness and anger twisted together inside her. She almost blurted that out to Jillian, but kept it to herself. The last thing she wanted to do was spoil her friend's happy day. She and Brody had waited a long time and gone through a lot finally to be together. No way would Mattie rain on their parade.

She sat on the brick step beside her friend and rested her hands on Jillian's chair arm, her chin on her linked fingers. ''How about this?'' she asked. ''You and Brody take your vows first. We'll go through the whole ceremony, take pictures, everything. I'll disappear to change into my...traditional wedding outfit.

While I'm doing that, my uncle can make an announcement that there will be another wedding. It will be like two separate ceremonies, but we'll share guests and a reception.''

"That's a wonderful idea," Jillian said.

"Are you sure it's all right with you?"

"I'm positive." Jillian's face brightened even more as she spotted Brody and Dawson approaching. "Look who's here. Speak of the devils."

"You got that right," Mattie said under her breath as she watched her fiancé walk toward them.

"What did you say?" Jillian asked.

"I said, 'What a sight we'll be.'"

When the men joined them, Mattie noted the sparkle of anticipation in Brody's eyes as he leaned down to kiss his wife-to-be. He caressed her rounded belly tenderly. "How are you?" he asked.

"Fine and dandy." Jillian smiled lovingly at him.

Mattie looked at Dawson and wondered what he was thinking as he watched the devoted couple. His look gave nothing away. "So how did it go with Uncle Ryan?" she asked as brightly as she could.

"You mean, when I asked him for your hand in marriage?" Dawson said.

"Is that what you did?" she asked.

Studying his expression, she did not find even a trace of humor. He was completely serious. There was something so old-fashioned and courtly about the gesture of asking permission from the senior male in the family that it warmed her heart. The whole affair seemed so passionless and she needed so badly to discover some hint of warmth, spirit, meaning—soul.

"You asked Uncle Ryan for permission to marry me?" she repeated.

"He sure did." Brody grinned. "Said that since Dad and Mom are so far away, Ryan is the next in line, and he asked permission to make you his wife."

"And?" Mattie asked.

Brody shrugged. "You're over twenty-one. What was he going to say?"

"It's about darn time." Mattie threw up her hands. "I've been trying for ages to make everyone recognize that I'm a mature woman."

"He also said that he will pull strings and call in favors if necessary to push through the paperwork for a marriage license," Dawson replied.

Brody kissed her cheek. "Congratulations, sis. Dawson's a good man. This is pretty sudden, but when it's right, it's right. No point in fighting it. Jillian and I tried that and it didn't work."

Mattie narrowed her gaze on Dawson and wondered what he'd said to her brother. How had he convinced him it was right? Somehow she had a sneaking suspicion that it was practically word for word what she'd told Jillian. And for the same reason—to preserve the happiness of their day.

"Yes, indeed," she said. "Three days from now we'll all be saying, 'I do.'"

Ten

Clutching her bouquet of baby's breath, carnations and marigolds, Mattie stood in the great room and looked through the French doors to the courtyard that was filling with guests. Everyone was waiting until stragglers arrived for the one o'clock wedding and were seated. Then Brody and Jillian's ceremony would start. She looked at the cloudless blue sky in the distance and was grateful that it was a beautiful day for a wedding. And that her parents wouldn't witness her wedding, what would not be her happiest day.

They had practically just returned to Australia from Reed and Mallory's nuptials. Brody and Jillian planned to visit when they could after the baby was born. Although a little sad, Mattie was relieved too. Her mother would see through her like no one else could.

That was one less thing to worry about.

Three days earlier, Mattie hadn't been prepared for the level of terror that awaited her in this spot. So many kinds of terror, too. Like high heels. She glanced down at the hunter-green satin toes of her shoes that matched her velvet bridesmaid's dress. She was used to jeans and boots. What if she tripped walking between the rows of chairs where the guests sat? What if the crown of flowers encircling her head fell off while the ceremony was going on? What if she had a coughing attack? Or worse, a sneeze, and her nose started to run? What if she embarrassed her brother on the most important day of his life?

And that was just for starters. Then came the part when it would be the biggest day of *her* life.

Which brought her down her long list of terrors to Dawson Prescott. Or, more specifically, to marrying him. She was almost grateful to the terror that pumped adrenaline through her, because she'd hardly slept in three days. At least the panic kept her eyes open.

She had the strongest urge to run far and fast, but two things stopped her. No way would she let Brody and Jillian down and spoil their special day. Although she supposed she could go through their ceremony and then run like hell. But that wouldn't work because no way would she let her parents down, either. As Dawson would say, that was "unacceptable."

"How are you doing?"

Dawson. Without turning around, Mattie knew it was him. She knew his calm, steady voice, so deep that it raised tingles on her skin from head to toe. He stood behind her, so close that she could smell the intoxicating scent of his aftershave, hear his even breathing, feel the warmth from his body. Part of her wanted to savor it, wrap herself in it because she was cold from the inside out. Part of her wanted to tell him to back off because he was the reason she was cold.

But she didn't say anything. Later he would get what he deserved.

She turned around and was unprepared for the spectacular view of him in a traditional black tuxedo, white, pleated dress shirt with black studs marching down his chest, and bow tie, perfectly knotted at his neck. His sun-streaked hair was neatly combed. He was so handsome that he took her breath away. Not only that, but for a few moments she completely forgot to be mad at him.

There was a gleam in his eyes as he looked her over, from the top of her head, down the length of her dress, to the tips of her shoes peeking out from beneath her hem. His gaze met hers and there was an intensity in it that sent excitement skimming through her.

"You look beautiful," he said, his voice a shade huskier than just a moment before.

"So do you," she blurted out.

"Thanks." He grinned, and her heart started tap dancing.

"Don't let it go to your head," she grumbled, reminding herself that she was not happy with him. "I'm sure it's the clothes."

"You're still mad." It wasn't a question.

She shrugged. "Even if I wasn't, I still think it's the clothes."

"Is Jillian ready?" he asked, apparently deciding to retreat.

Mattie nodded. "Amy's with her." At his blank look, she said, "Amy Fairaday, Jillian's sister. She's the maid of honor and seems to be doing a fine job of keeping the bride calm."

"That's good," he said.

"Yup. Jill is as cool as a cucumber." She looked at him and realized he looked pretty cool, too, in view of what they faced. Then she wondered about her brother. "What about Brody?"

"Reed is with him, since he's the best man. I picked him and Mallory up at the airport this morning and brought them here, to the ranch. Since I had to be here anyway."

She ignored his casual reference to their impending nuptials. She didn't want to think about it until it was absolutely necessary. "Did they have a good trip?" She avoided using the word *honeymoon*. It would evoke too many erotic images that she couldn't deal with at the moment. She was already in hot water herself for putting the "wedding night" before the wedding.

"They said their honeymoon couldn't have been more perfect."

So much for avoiding the word. Leave it to Dawson. She was about to ask if he'd said anything to her brother and his sister about their surprise, when there was a commotion behind them. Jillian moved through the great room, decked out in her wedding finery and looking more beautiful than Mattie had ever seen her. She'd opted for a simple, floor-length, cream-colored dress with loose lines that minimized the appearance of her pregnancy. Her veil was anchored by a halo wreath of flowers in her straight, shoulder-length blond hair. The look was uncomplicated, yet delicately feminine.

Her sister was beside her. Amy was a little taller than Jillian, with the same coloring, blond and beautiful. "Brody has taken his place in the courtyard beside the justice of the peace. I think we're ready to start, sis," she said. She looked at the assembled group like a general surveying his troops. "Everyone know what to do? Mattie and Dawson go first."

Mattie nodded, even as her heart pounded so hard she thought it might pop from her chest. During rehearsal the night before, it had been decided that ushers and bridesmaids would walk together down the aisle.

Dawson cleared his throat. "Break a leg, kid."

"Oh, Lord, I hope not," she cried.

"It's just an expression. It means 'Good luck.'"

"I knew that," she said.

He held out his arm, and Mattie placed her shaking hand in the bend of his elbow. When he reached out and covered her cold fingers with his warm palm, she found the gesture surprisingly comforting. Mattie would have denied it from one end of the huge state of Texas to the other, but she was terribly grateful for Dawson's presence. She gripped her bouquet in her other hand and nodded that she was ready.

"Let's go," he said, opening the French doors.

He signaled to the quartet of musicians in the far corner of the courtyard. Instantly they stopped the chamber music they'd been playing, adjusted the sheet music on their stands, and started the traditional wedding march. The guests swiveled in their chairs to watch the procession, all of them smiling indulgently.

As she walked by, Mattie saw Dawson's sister, Mallory, and didn't miss the surprised look on her face. At first she wondered if her bra strap were showing, or if there were a spot on her dress. She stumbled slightly and felt Dawson's arm tense as he slowed to let her regain her balance.

Dawson bent and whispered in her ear. "Mallory hasn't seen you since the transformation."

She nodded, grateful for his support, yet at the same time angry that she was grateful to him for anything. She looked at him, trying to read the expression in his hazel eyes. Was he thinking about the fact that a little while from now, the two of them would be taking this same walk to become man and wife?

Before she could give that too much thought, they

reached the flower-covered arch where her two brothers stood beside the justice of the peace dressed in a black robe. She released Dawson's arm and walked to the left, while he took his place beside the groom and best man on the right. She turned and watched the rest of the bridal procession.

She quickly glanced at Jillian, then swung her gaze to see the look on Brody's face. Her heart caught at the look of admiration, awe, wonder, and most of all love, that was in his eyes. Then a feeling of sadness enveloped her. How she'd always hoped that the man she married would look at her like that.

But it wasn't to be.

When the bridal couple were together in front of the arbor, arm in arm, the ceremony began. Different friends and relatives that Jillian and Brody had chosen ahead of time read inspirational pieces about devotion, love, soul mates, and happily-ever-after. Each one was like a knife through Mattie's heart.

Finally, the bride and groom faced each other and joined hands. They each made promises that they'd written themselves. Then the justice of the peace had them repeat the traditional vows to love, honor and cherish. Finally, he beamed at Brody and said, "You may kiss your bride."

"With pleasure," Brody said. He molded Jillian against him with one arm, then cupped her cheek with his hand and lowered his mouth to hers. The kiss seemed to go on and on, until hoots and catcalls from the guests forced the laughing couple to separate.

"Ladies and gentlemen," the judge said, "may I present to you Mr. and Mrs. Brody Fortune."

Applause filled the courtyard. Sadness and guilt filled Mattie's heart. She was glad her brother and Jillian had finally found each other. At the same time, she was so envious of their happiness that she could hardly stand it. It was such a stark contrast to the punishment she faced of marrying a man who didn't love her.

Jillian and Brody walked back among their guests. Amy took Reed's arm and moved away from the arbor. Then Dawson was beside her, and she felt the rush of hummingbird wings inside her that she was beginning to associate with his closeness. As they entered the house, she heard the judge, still standing in front of the arbor, ask for everyone's attention. He asked the guests to stay in their seats; he had a surprise announcement from the family. When he finished, voices rose to an excited buzz.

Here it comes, she thought. *My turn.* With every ounce of willpower in her body, she held back the tears that burned her eyes.

Dawson stood beside the justice of the peace, waiting for Mattie to open the French doors and walk down the aisle to join him. Griff had agreed to be his best man, mostly, Dawson was sure, to make certain they went through with the wedding.

Scanning the gathered guests, he spotted Mallory. After he'd brought her to the ranch from the airport, he'd confided to her that he was getting married. He'd braced himself for her attempt to talk him out of making the biggest mistake of his life. Surprisingly, she'd hugged him and said she wasn't shocked in the least. With all the sparks he and Mattie had set off the first time they'd laid eyes on each other, it had been a good thing it wasn't raining. Everyone at that rodeo would have been electrocuted by their love at first sight.

Sparks? Love at first sight?

Dawson didn't believe in it. But if romantic notions kept his sister happy, far be it from him to set her straight. Suddenly he felt Griff stiffen, and he looked up in time to see Willa Simms come through the French doors.

"I didn't know Mattie asked Willa to stand up with her," Griff whispered to him.

Dawson met his gaze. "Probably because Mattie is giving you the silent treatment."

"True enough." He nodded grimly. "Did you know about Willa?"

"Mattie's giving me the silent treatment too," he said. "I knew they became friends while both of them were here on the ranch. But the renovations on her apartment in College Station were completed and recently she moved in. I didn't know Mattie had talked to her."

"When did Willa move?"

Dawson shrugged. "About a week ago, I guess."

"She's not wearing her glasses," Griff observed.

Dawson studied her. In her ankle-length peach gown with matching jacket, she looked very pretty. Her auburn hair was pulled up at the crown, and curls spilled down, with wisps framing her face. She smiled shyly as she walked. When she reached the arbor, her gaze was on Griff, and there was a sparkle in her eyes. The judge indicated where she should stand, since she hadn't been there for the previous evening's rehearsal.

Then Dawson fixed his gaze on the French doors. Knowing how close she was to her family, he felt badly that this had moved too quickly for them to come. On the other hand, they were protected from details he would rather they not know. His heart

pounded as he waited expectantly for Mattie. He didn't
know how she could top the beautiful picture she'd
made in her bridesmaid's dress. She had bowled him
over. But he found that the thought of seeing her walk
gracefully toward him to become his wife made his
palms sweat and his heart race.

When she appeared in the doorway, Dawson was
stunned. Instead of the white dress and veil he'd expected, she was wearing her jeans, boots and denim
shirt. The guests whispered to each other, replacing
the astonished silence her appearance had caused.
With chin held high, she moved down the aisle, a
smile plastered on her face. The seductive sway of her
hips kicked his heart into double time. His gaze lowered to the shapely curves of her thighs and calves.
Not until that moment had he realized how much he'd
missed the sight of her long, slender legs, which had
been hidden by her floor-length dress.

When she reached him, they assumed their places
before the judge, who removed the glasses from his
nose and stared at her. "I thought you were going to
change," he said.

"Yes, sir. I did."

"For your wedding," he added.

"I know," she answered, nodding.

"But you're wearing jeans." The justice of the
peace gazed from the toes of her scuffed boots to her
jeans. They were so worn and soft that they were almost threadbare at the pressure points, Dawson noted,
which also happened to be where she was curvy. The
thought made his mouth go dry and his blood pressure
jump a couple of notches.

"Your Honor, I train horses for a living. This is
who I really am." She angled her head toward Daw-

son. "Makeup and a fancy dress got his attention. But he needs to know what he's getting into."

The judge sighed. "My wife would say that marriage to a man is a lot like training a horse," he said.

She grinned. "I'm glad you see my point."

"Although some take to the reins better than others," he added, glancing at Dawson.

"Remember what they say," Dawson interjected.

"What's that?" Mattie and the judge asked in unison.

"You can't teach an *old* dog new tricks." Dawson knew she got the double meaning, even if the judge didn't.

Mattie glared at him as he took her hand, but didn't pull away. Instead she whispered, "Make no mistake, Dawson, you can't make a silk purse from a sow's ear. What you see is what you get."

"Okay."

She looked momentarily taken aback. "So you still want to go through with this?"

"Absolutely. I wouldn't change a hair on your head or anything else about you," he said, glancing down at her denim shirt, at the point where the snaps closed just above her breasts.

He'd been half kidding, but Dawson was surprised to realize that what he'd told her was true. In front of God and everyone present, she'd made it clear what her feelings were. He admired her fearless spirit and total honesty. He also saw the insecurity lurking in her eyes. She wasn't as tough as she pretended. He would do his best to protect her tender heart from hurt.

"All right, then," she said. "Let's get this show on the road."

The judge cleared his throat. "Dearly beloved, we

are still gathered before God to unite *this* man and *this* woman in holy matrimony.''

"Can we just skip to the 'I dos?'" Mattie asked him.

The judge raised one white eyebrow. "You don't want all the trimmings?"

"Do I look like an all-the-trimmings kind of woman?"

He gave her attire another once-over and sighed. "Good point." He met Dawson's gaze and shook his head sympathetically. "Son, you've got your work cut out for you."

"Truer words were never spoken," Dawson said.

"What about me?" she asked indignantly. "Don't you think I've got my work cut out for me? Haven't you ever heard the saying— You can't judge a dog by its spots? Your Honor, you don't know what a trial *he* can be," she said, cocking her thumb in Dawson's direction. Then she realized what she'd said and chuckled at her pun. "A little legal humor."

The justice looked taken aback. "Frankly, I'm not exactly sure what to think about the two of you. As a favor to your uncle Ryan, I'm not going to walk out. So let's do this wedding before I change my mind."

"She'll behave," Dawson said, hoping it was true. He knew her behavior was calculated to make him change his mind. If anything, it made him want her more. For the life of him, he hadn't a clue why.

The judge looked at them sternly, then said, "Do you, Dawson Geoffrey Prescott—"

"Geoffrey?" Mattie whispered.

"My father's name," Dawson whispered.

He couldn't help thinking how appropriate it was to have a reminder of his reasons for marrying Mattie.

He might have his father's name, but no way was he as unfeeling and irresponsible as the man whose blood ran through his veins.

"—take this woman for your lawful wife," the judge continued, ignoring their exchange.

"I do," Dawson said, loudly and clearly.

"Do you Matilda Theodora—"

"Theodora?" Dawson repeated, raising an eyebrow.

"My father's name," she said.

"—take this man," the judge continued, frowning at them as if they were two recalcitrant children.

"I do." She mumbled something else that sounded an awful lot like *under protest,* But Dawson knew no one else could hear it and it was for his ears alone.

The judge looked at them over the glasses perched on the end of his nose and said, "Then with the authority granted to me by the glorious state of Texas, I pronounce you husband and wife." He met Dawson's gaze. "And may God have mercy on you."

"Amen to that," Dawson said. Then he took Mattie in his arms and thoroughly kissed his bride as he'd been wanting to all day.

Dawson and Mattie were in the study with Ryan, Griff and Willa. While her aunt Lily was seeing to the guests at the reception, they were gathered to make sure the wedding paperwork was in order before the judge left.

Now her uncle handed each of them a glass of champagne. "I propose a toast," he said. "To Dawson, a man I've come to think of as a son. Now you're officially a member of the family. And my niece, Mattie. In a short time, you've become more like a daughter to me. May your life together be filled with adventure, laughter, and most of all, love.''

''To Mattie and Dawson,'' they chorused.

As Mattie sipped, she thought about her uncle's toast. Adventure was good. Laughter, probably. She figured she and Dawson might be able to manage that. His reaction to her wedding attire had encouraged her on that score. He looked very surprised but not at all angry or upset, as she'd expected. Amused was more how she would describe his response. But love? She hoped so.

At least on Dawson's part. She studied Dawson, so handsome in his tuxedo. Her pulse quickened as she observed his square jaw and wide shoulders. Yet there was gentleness in him as he held the crystal flute. And the way he'd made love to her... So considerate. And he'd been angry that she hadn't told him she was a virgin so that he could have taken better care. The thought started a glow in the center of her abdomen and radiated outward.

Now they were husband and wife, and it was legal to make love anytime. Anticipation filled her at the idea of being close to him again.

More than that, she planned to do her best to find love with him. The only way she'd been able to force herself to walk down that aisle was her determination to try and make him love her. She realized that her prank attire probably hadn't been putting her best boot forward. But his response had encouraged her. Maybe he wasn't as much of a stuffed shirt as she'd thought. And if she tried very hard, she could be his helpmate in life. Maybe love would follow.

Dawson held up his glass. ''My thanks to Griff for being my best man.''

"You're welcome," Griff answered gruffly. "I wouldn't have put on this monkey suit for anyone but Mattie."

If he hadn't meddled, she thought, he wouldn't have had to dress up at all. Sniffing over his attempt at diplomacy, Mattie held up her glass. "I propose a toast to Willa. Thanks for standing up with me on such short notice."

Willa tucked a strand of auburn hair behind her ear and clinked Mattie's glass. "It was my pleasure. I'm so happy to be included in all your family gatherings. Dad and Ryan became best friends in Vietnam. Since my father passed away two years ago, I've missed him terribly. He would be happy knowing I'm not alone. It's wonderful to be around people." She glanced shyly at Griff.

Well, well, Mattie thought. *She's got an eye for my brother. The big lug doesn't deserve her.* At least not until Mattie got over being mad at him for forcing Dawson to marry her. How long would it take before she would forgive him? As long as it took for Dawson to fall in love with her. And that could take a very long time.

Mattie pushed aside her feelings and smiled at Willa. "You're like family, Willa. So tell me about your apartment. Is the redecorating completed?"

The other woman sipped thoughtfully and nodded. "It's fine. I love the area and can't wait to start teaching."

Mattie thought she detected some reserve in her friend, and wondered if she should say anything. "Well, I'm glad. And especially grateful that you could be here with me today."

"I'm glad you called me."

"That reminds me," Mattie said. Things had been a whirlwind and she had forgotten to bring up something that had bothered her since that call to her friend. She decided to say something, and they could all tell her she was a worrywart. "You sounded funny the other night when we talked on the phone. Is everything all right?"

Willa nodded, a bit too emphatically. "Fine. It's just…"

"What?" Griff asked, a note of concern in his voice.

Mattie frowned. Her brother, too, sensed that something wasn't quite right with Willa.

The other woman shrugged. "When Mattie called, I almost didn't answer."

"Why?" Griff said, the concern cranking up a notch.

"It's too stupid to bring up."

Uncle Ryan sipped his champagne. "Nothing is too stupid to bring up. Especially while Clint Lockhart is still at large."

"I've been getting calls." Willa shrugged. "But I'm just being a baby. It's a new place. I'm all by myself. Strange sounds. I just have to get used to it."

"Maybe," Dawson said. "But Ryan's right. With Clint out there, you can't be too careful."

"What kind of calls?" Griff asked.

She looked at the three men, anxiety in her blue-gray eyes. "Hang-ups all times of the day and night. It's the ones that wake me from a sound sleep that are the most disturbing. I can hear someone breathing on the other end of the phone, but no one says anything."

Ryan put his glass on the desk. "Damn it. Clint Lockhart."

"Are you sure it's a man?" Dawson asked.

"I have no idea." Willa shook her head. "No one ever says anything."

"It's Clint. He hasn't been apprehended," Ryan said, his words humming with anger. "I talked to Sheriff Grayhawk before the wedding. Clint's eluded law enforcement, just dropped out of sight. They think someone's hiding him."

"But how would he know where Willa lives? And why would he target her, anyway?" Mattie asked.

"Who knows how he finds out anything?" Ryan answered, his voice curt with frustration. "As far as targets, his mind is so whacked, I don't think he's discriminating. He wants to get me. He'll do that by hurting anyone I care about. Security here on the ranch is tight, and he can't get to anyone here. So..." He shrugged, letting the disturbing thought spin out.

Mattie noticed that Griff shifted closer to Willa when the other woman shivered at the words.

Ryan looked at Griff. "I want you to do a security check on Willa's phone and the rest of her apartment."

Griff moved his shoulders restlessly, as if he wasn't comfortable in his own skin. "Yes, sir. But are you sure I'm the right man—"

"You're a Fortune. You're the best at your job." Ryan nodded. "I can trust you with my godchild's safety. You're definitely the right man."

Willa's cheeks turned a becoming shade of pink. "Are you sure that's necessary? I don't think Clint would do anything to me."

Ryan shook his head angrily. "Until he's behind bars again, the whole Fortune family is at risk." He looked at Dawson. "That goes for you, too. Mattie's your responsibility now. My niece's safety is in your hands. She's your wife.''

"I'll take good care of her, sir," Dawson said.

His wife. Mattie shivered at the thought.

"Good." Ryan walked to the door. "I suggest we go out and mingle with everyone. Jillian and Brody planned to stay for a little while, then head out on their honeymoon. Don't want to miss them." He looked from Dawson to Mattie, who squirmed under his look. "What about you two? Any plans for a trip?"

Dawson glanced at her as he hesitated a moment. She refused to jump in and help him. This was his idea; he could field the difficult questions.

Finally he said, "Mattie and I had such a whirlwind courtship, and jumping into the wedding while Mallory and Reed were still here in the States, we want to catch our breath. We'll take our time and think about a honeymoon."

Good save, Dawson, she thought. She had to give him credit. He was smooth.

"Sounds wise," Ryan said as he walked through the doorway.

Willa and Dawson followed him. Mattie started after them, but Griff stopped her with a hand on her arm. "Mattie, I'm not sure I can handle the security job at Willa's."

"Why?"

There was worry in his brown eyes, making them darker than usual; his lips tightened as he looked at her. "She's such a lady. And I'm—" He shrugged. "You know, rough around the edges. I think Ryan should find someone else to check out her place."

The vulnerability Mattie saw in his eyes punctured

her bubble of anger, which flew off like a deflating balloon. She touched his arm. "You're exactly the right man to do the job—for all the reasons Uncle Ryan said. Besides, I think Willa's got a crush on you."

He reached out and felt her forehead. "No fever. Guess marriage has already done a number on you."

She laughed. "Okay. Don't listen to me. But you're right about marriage. It's a scary proposition."

Griff encircled her shoulders and pulled her against him in a quick hug. "I have a feeling everything is going to work out fine."

"From your mouth to God's ear," she whispered fervently.

The thought of being Mrs. Dawson Prescott brought to mind a whole lot of apprehension. It had nothing to do with Clint Lockhart—and everything to do with whether or not she could find love with her husband.

Eleven

Dawson stopped his BMW at the gate to his Kingston Estates home, lowered the driver's window and punched several buttons on a keypad. The next thing Mattie knew, the wrought-iron gate, part of the brick-capped wall that surrounded his property, whispered open.

"This is it," he said, guiding the car up the long drive that curved to the left before stopping in front of the house. There was unmistakable pride in his voice, and from the little she could see of the impressive structure in the dark, he had every right to feel that way.

"It's really something," she answered.

Mattie was almost grateful for not sleeping much since becoming engaged to Dawson. Lack of rest, combined with nonstop wedding preparations had made her numb. She wasn't sure how to feel, which was probably a good thing. She was almost beyond feeling anything at all. The clock on the car's dashboard showed midnight. The optimum hour to begin her fairy tale. Or end it.

She would assume her role as Dawson's wife—with all the fringe benefits. Like sharing his bed. The thought made her shiver with anticipation, and she realized that maybe she wasn't as tired as she'd thought.

Another blissful night in his arms would make all the stress worth it.

He turned the car's ignition off and the engine died, along with the interior dash lights. She glanced to her right and noticed that the planters across the whole front of the house, including the walkway, were rimmed with small lights.

"I never saw lights with little hats on before," she said. "They're cute."

He got out of the car and walked around to her side, looking tense in the dim light from the open door. "I'm glad you like them, but cute isn't their primary function."

"Heaven forbid they're just decorative. What might their primary function be?"

"This lot is two acres, and the house is set pretty far back, away from the street and the lights. The cute little guys illuminate the walkway so you don't trip and break your neck," he answered. He didn't sound angry, so much as tired and uptight.

"And a worthy service they provide," she agreed.

Dawson opened the trunk and lifted out the several suitcases she'd packed. They had agreed she would get the rest of her things from the ranch later. He hefted her bags and led the way past the house's stone-work facade up the steps to the raised-panel oak door. Leaded, beveled glass decorated the center panel. With interior lights on, this door would be breathtakingly beautiful, she thought as Dawson unlocked and opened it.

He reached past her and flipped on the entryway light, then let her precede him into the house. The odor of fresh paint tickled her nose. At least he hadn't lied to her about that.

But as she surveyed her new home, something about the place left her vaguely uneasy. She couldn't put a finger on why.

"The house is trilevel," Dawson explained.

They had walked straight into the living room, which had high ceilings and a bay window. He led her up a half-flight of stairs. "This is the formal dining room, kitchen and family room." He set her bags down there.

"It's beautiful," she said, meaning it. She walked past the huge oak table and hutch in the dining room and leaned over the oak railing to peer down into the living room. "Really impressive," she said.

But something about it still disturbed her.

She met him in the family room, where the furniture consisted of a leather couch and love seat set at a right angle to each other. They were arranged in front of the brick fireplace. Lamps were made of wrought-iron and wood. In spite of the expensive furnishings, the room felt spartan, without pictures on the walls or framed photographs on the mantel. In the corner of the vast area sat the biggest television set she had ever seen. The ceiling was dotted with grids that she assumed were speakers for a sound system.

Dawson apparently noticed where she was looking. "State-of-the-art surround sound," he said proudly. "It will make you feel like you're at the movies."

"Lovely," she answered. "Vibrating from the outside in."

"The master bedroom is this way," he said, pointing down the hall before leading the way.

Her heart started to pound as she followed. *The bedroom I will share with my husband.* He flipped on the light, illuminating a huge room dominated by a king-size bed covered with a black comforter. The oak headboard reminded Mattie of an entertainment center and took up almost one wall. It was a series of sliding doors, drawers and cupboards. In her fairy tale, the bed had always been a megaromantic four-poster. Except when she was about seventeen and she thought waterbeds were the best thing since sliced bread. But this bed was certainly big enough for a married couple to explore each other. She shivered with excitement.

The bathroom had two sinks with gold fixtures, and a stall shower. What fascinated her most was the whirlpool bath, which looked as if it would hold the two of them very comfortably, even though Dawson was a big man. The thought sent a flash-fire of sensation sweeping over her body. The walk-in closet was the size of a bedroom and was filled with Dawson's suits, ties, dress shirts, shoes, jeans and boots. Big as it was, all the hanging space was used.

He showed her two more bedrooms. One was set up with a computer desk, fax machine, copy machine, and telephones—obviously a home office. The other had gym equipment—weight bench, exercise cycle, treadmill, and other gizmos with weights, cables and handles that looked to her like torture devices left over from the Spanish Inquisition.

Next he led her to the bottom and final level of the house. It featured a great room with more leather furniture, a spare room for storage, and another bedroom that opened onto the brick-trimmed patio and pool area.

After showing her everything, Dawson led the way back up the half-flight of stairs to the family room. He rested his hands on his hips and swung his gaze around the room proudly.

"So what do you think of it?" he asked.

"I think the floor plan is wonderful," she answered sincerely. But the whole place left her feeling cold and unwelcome. Every room he'd shown her had made her more and more uneasy. But why? "The rooms are large with lots of windows. It's huge."

"So which bedroom do you want?" he asked.

Uh-oh. "What did you say?" she asked, unable to believe her ears.

"I asked which room you want. The way the house is laid out, it's like having two master suites. Since they're on separate floors, we can both have our privacy."

She stared at him. "Privacy?"

Disappointment filled her. She'd always thought married people slept in the same room. Her parents did. Uncle Ryan and Aunt Lily did. She'd bet her favorite saddle that none of her married brothers, and even the ones who *weren't* hitched, slept in a bed separate from their significant other. Her one and only experience had shown her it was one of the marriage perks.

"Privacy?" she asked again.

"Yeah. The master gives you kitchen privileges. But downstairs is easily accessible to the pool and whirlpool bath outside. Both floors have a family room. It will work out great."

Great if you want to avoid someone, she thought. *Great if you want to dodge, elude, escape or flee from the woman you just married. Great if you want privacy.*

Finally she got what had been bothering her since walking into his house. The unmistakable signs of new paint were there. The rest of the house shouted No

Women Allowed. He didn't want a wife. He didn't want a woman to share his life. He didn't want to be married. In fact, he looked as miserable as she felt.

She might have worked up some pity for him, except she had the unshakable sense that even if Griff hadn't pushed the issue, Dawson would have. He felt obligated to marry her because he'd been responsible for taking her virginity—even though she'd slept with him because she wanted to. And as much as she might want to hand all the blame to Griff and Dawson for this marriage, she couldn't. If she hadn't felt there was a small chance for happiness, she would have faced her family, confessed what she'd done, and taken her lumps. She married Dawson with every hope that they could make this relationship work.

But the truth was, Dawson didn't want her.

He ran a hand through his hair. "Look, Mattie, we both know this isn't a real marriage. You agreed under duress, and I want you to know that I don't expect…anything."

Mattie was tired, more so than she'd ever been in her life. And every fiber of her being was focused on one thing: not letting the tears burning the backs of her eyes fall. She didn't have the energy to figure out how she felt about this. She was too tired to argue. She was too tired to be angry. Unfortunately, there was one emotion she wasn't too tired to feel. Profound sadness.

"I'll take the master bedroom," she said. She wasn't too tired to want this to be as difficult, annoying and inconvenient for him as possible. He might put her in another room, but he wouldn't be able to ignore her presence.

"Okay. I'll put your suitcases in there." He picked

them up. "Do you mind if I move my stuff out in the morning?"

"Not at all," she said.

She didn't care if he moved it or left it. She didn't care about much at that moment—except that he not see how very much he had hurt her.

Dawson cut through the water in the pool, kicking and stroking his way from one end to the other. He added more laps. The swim had felt good. He'd needed the exercise. Translation: He wanted Mattie more than he'd wanted any woman—ever. He'd never experienced a more hellish night. A night spent tossing, turning and thinking about Mattie. And he'd awakened in an acute state of need. The cold water and the cold late-November air, he'd hoped, would take the edge off his tension.

But he was still strung tighter than a brand-new fiddle. He couldn't get the expression on her face out of his mind. She'd looked like a kid who'd just been told there was no Santa Claus, Tooth Fairy, or Easter Bunny—all at the same time. She was crushed. It was as if all the animation, energy and joy had gone out of her.

And he was responsible.

He knew in his gut, though, that keeping her at arm's length was the right thing. Although he wanted her in his bed almost more than he wanted his next breath, separate rooms was his punishment to bear for taking advantage of her naiveté. It would never happen again. He'd sunk to his father's level. The first chance he'd gotten, he'd used her innocence and seduced her.

He'd made one mistake, but he wouldn't compound it by turning his back on her *or* renewing their intimate relationship. He wasn't worthy of her love. And using her that way would only hurt her more in the long run. Someday she would understand that he'd done this for her.

His muscles ached from the exertion of his swim, and he hauled himself out of the pool and picked up a towel.

"She'll thank me for keeping the distance between us," he mumbled to himself as he dried off. "Yeah, when pigs fly." He laughed, a bitter, hollow sound, as he slung the towel across his shoulders.

"How long are you gonna stand there talking to yourself?"

He whirled around and looked up at Mattie, bent over and resting her elbows on the balcony outside the kitchen.

"You're up early," he said, grinning in spite of himself at the saucy picture she made. Oversize T-shirt that said Dallas Cowboys on the front. Black sweatpants slightly pulled up to reveal slender ankles and bare feet. Barefoot and pregnant. The thought made his blood run cold. Naw. Couldn't happen. It had only been one time. He took a deep breath.

"I always get up at the crack of dawn," she said. "Do you want some breakfast?" She angled her head toward the room behind her. "I've got bacon, eggs, pancakes, hash browns."

"I didn't know you could cook."

"You still don't know that I can. I could be lying about the food. I could be telling the truth about the cooking part, but consuming it might take the constitution of a garbage truck. Why don't you come on up here and see for yourself whether or not I'm telling the truth."

"All right, you're on. Give me a couple of minutes to shower. And I'll be right up."

"The clock is ticking." She turned around and went back inside.

Anticipation hummed through him as he quickly showered and dried off. He put on sweats and a T-shirt, the only clothes he'd brought downstairs last night. He would need to dress for work soon. He'd been neglecting things at the office.

When he walked into the kitchen, the delicious smells made his mouth water. Almost as much as did the sight of Mattie—blond hair tucked behind her ears, cheeks pink from her culinary exertions, gray eyes shining as she stood by the stove watching the bubbles on her pancakes pop.

She flipped them over. "I hope you're hungry."

"Starved," he said, his gaze lowering to her long legs.

"The table is set. Take a seat, and I'll bring everything over when these are done."

He noticed the drip coffeemaker waited with a full, fresh pot. "Would you like some coffee?" he asked.

"I don't drink it," she said, glancing over her shoulder at him. "I just figured since you had the contraption, you probably did. I found the can of coffee in the fridge and made a pot."

"It smells great."

And so do you, he thought as they stood shoulder to shoulder. She flipped flapjacks, while he poured himself coffee. Domestic as hell.

And he realized he liked it.

He thought back, and realized that no woman had ever made him breakfast before. At least not in his house. No woman had stayed overnight before. It was his rule, because he never wanted a woman to feel used. Now he had a wife. She had made him breakfast. Inside, he was grinning like the fool he no doubt was.

"Sit down," she said again. "Everything is ready."

He took his seat across from the slider that looked out on the balcony. The table was set for two, with the green, woven placemats and matching cloth napkins that Mallory had sent him for a housewarming gift. Juice was poured and the center of the table was filled with jars and bottles that contained syrup, butter, ketchup, Tabasco, salsa.

Mattie brought him a plate piled with hash browns, bacon, eggs, pancakes and wheat toast. Ruefully she inspected the lack of room on the table as she set the food in front of him.

"I found all this in the refrigerator, but I didn't know what you liked. So I put it all out."

Sort of like she did with everything. Put it out there, and what you see is what you get. He admired that about her. No pretense. No games. Pure honesty.

"Thanks, Mattie. It looks great. Smells even better."

"This is the moment of truth," she said, filling a plate for herself. She sat down at a right angle to him. "Now you get to judge whether or not I'm a good cook."

He found he was hungry. After putting butter and syrup on the flapjacks, he tasted a bite. It melted in his mouth. He sampled some of everything and said, "This tastes good."

She smiled. "I'm glad."

They ate in silence for a few moments. Finally Dawson said, "Where did you learn to cook like this?"

"My mother." She ate a forkful of eggs. "With all of us kids and Dad to feed, she always needed a hand in the kitchen. I picked it up by osmosis, I guess."

"I figured you were always out in the north forty with the horses."

She shrugged. "I did that, too."

He realized that they hadn't had an opportunity to discuss what she would do after they got married.

"Horses have always been a big part of your life?" he asked.

She nodded as she nibbled on a piece of toast. "For as far back as I can remember. I can't imagine not training horses."

"You live a long way from the ranch now."

"Not that far. I worked it out before the wedding yesterday."

"You did?"

She nodded. "Ethan offered to pick me up. Uncle Ryan said I could use one of the ranch vehicles until we make other arrangements."

Cowboys. The thought tightened his gut like wet rawhide drying in the sun. His wife alone with a cowboy. He didn't like the idea of that. Not one single bit.

"I'll drive you to the ranch," he said.

She stopped nibbling and stared at him. "I have it worked out. It's not your problem."

"It's no trouble."

She glanced at the clock on the stove and jumped up. "Can we talk about this tonight?"

Tonight. The word conjured an image of twisted sheets with Mattie lying in the middle of them. Her hair tangled from his hands. Her mouth swollen from his kisses. Her body satisfied from his loving. Instantly he was hard and ready. If he was going to keep his distance from her, that was a bad sign.

"I'm not sure what time I'll be home," he said.

The light in her eyes, so bright only moments before, seemed to flicker and go out. "I've got to change. Ethan will be here any minute." She hurried from the room.

He stared for a long time at her half-eaten food. "Someday you'll thank me, Mattie."

As she'd walked down the aisle to him, he'd seen through her bluster to the tender heart beneath. He'd promised to keep her from hurt, even if he was the potential source of that hurt.

Twelve

Mattie mulled over the events of the last week. They'd settled into a daily routine, except for Thanksgiving Day. Ryan and Lily had invited them to the big family gathering on the ranch. She and Dawson had played newlyweds to the hilt. But as she put the finishing touches on the latest chicken recipe she was trying, she shook her head. She knew she was no closer to getting Dawson into her bed—or rather into his bed with her—than she'd been seven days ago. She'd played Hannah Homemaker long enough and was darn well ready for some payback.

"Gotta rattle his cage," she said to herself. "And I think I know just how to do it."

That morning she'd asked if there was any way she could have the car. They hadn't discussed getting another vehicle and the ranch truck she'd been using needed an overhaul. He'd arranged to ride to the office with his friend Zane. He and his wife Gwen also had a house in Kingston Estates, not far from Dawson's.

Mattie had done her wifely errands: a stop at the cleaner's to drop off his suits, at the grocery store. So much for the way to a man's heart being through his stomach. Apparently she needed to find the detour to Dawson's ticker. All week she'd been cooking semi-gourmet meals, but although he had nothing but praise for the results, he hadn't invited himself back into his own bed beside her.

She knew if their marriage stood a ghost of a chance for success, that had to happen. She'd also thought about doing the inviting, but was afraid her fragile ego couldn't handle a rejection. So on to Plan B: a *romantic* dinner.

Her purchases had included a bouquet of flowers for the table, along with scented candles. And a new outfit. That part had taken the longest. She'd found her way into Dawson's arms the first time with the help of a dynamite dress. This outfit had to be just right. Subtle, but sexy. Attention-getting, but seductive. Figure-flattering, but not too obvious.

She glanced at the sliding glass doors that acted as a mirror against the dark night outside. She'd chosen a white lounging outfit from a well-known lingerie store. The pants tied at the waist, were loose at the hip, but tapered to a crew band at the ankle. The matching short top had a scooped neckline to accentuate her breasts and show just a hint of cleavage, yet it skimmed her waist, flashing her midriff when she moved a certain way.

"I hope this does the trick," she said to herself.

She walked into the family room and surveyed the small table she'd set up in front of the fireplace. "Tablecloth, check. Flowers, check. Crystal wineglasses, check."

She took a long wooden match from the slender box beside the hearth and lit the gas fireplace. A cheerful blaze instantly ignited.

In the kitchen, she sprinkled cheese on the chicken dish, the final touch before sticking it in the oven. The question was how long to bake it. She glanced at the

clock and noted that it was five-thirty. Dawson had
been walking in the door from work earlier and earlier
every day. She hadn't a clue how to judge cooking
time to coordinate with his arrival. She put the dish in
the oven and hoped for the best. She'd done everything humanly possible to create a romantic atmo-
sphere. There was nothing more she could do, short
of greeting her husband at the door wearing nothing
but a smile.

The thought made her chuckle. She could probably
manage the nerve to do that, but hoped it wouldn't be
necessary. It would be so much more satisfying if
Dawson undressed her. The thought sent shivers over
her flesh.

An outside sound drifted to her, like a car door closing. She was still adjusting to the different noises of
a new house in the suburbs, and wasn't certain. Then
she heard the front door open and close.

"Dawson?"

"Yeah." He walked into the kitchen.

Mattie looked at him, white shirt with sleeves rolled
up to the elbow, tie at half-staff, suit coat slung over
his arm, briefcase in hand. Her insides quivered and
the blood raced through her veins. Who'd have
guessed that a rumpled executive instead of a Texas
cowboy would tug at her heart this way?

She moved around the center island work area to
where he stood on the other side. His eyes darkened,
and he started to lean toward her. A hi-honey-I'm-
home kiss? Lord, she hoped so. She would make it a
welcome-back-at-the-end-of-a-long-day kiss that he
wouldn't forget in a hurry.

But he seemed to catch himself, and he straightened.
He turned away and set his briefcase down.

"How was your day?" she asked. Isn't that what a wife said when her husband arrived home after work? Even if she didn't get a kiss? Sheer force of will kept her voice cheerful and her disappointment at bay.

He nodded. "Good. Profits are up in all areas of the business. We're considering an expansion in the real estate market. All in all, I'd say things are going well." Sniffing, he said, "I don't smell anything cooking."

That was a good sign, wasn't it? The fact that he expected food when he arrived home from work?

"You should soon. I just put dinner in the oven. I wasn't sure when you'd be home."

"I guess I should have called." He looked at the empty kitchen table. "I'll put out plates and utensils, if you want."

"I've already done it."

"I guess we're using the invisible china and flatware tonight?" He raised one eyebrow questioningly.

She laughed. "No. It's in the family room."

He turned to look, and she saw his shoulders tense when he spotted the candle-and-flower-bedecked table in front of the fireplace and the brightly burning blaze.

"Oh, I forgot something," she said.

"You could have fooled me," he answered, an edge to his voice.

She walked over to one of the cupboards and opened it, looking up for what she wanted. She could have sworn there was an ice bucket in there. She planned to keep the wine bottle chilled on the table. On the top shelf, she spotted what she was looking for, and lifted her arms in an attempt to get it down.

"Let me do that," Dawson said, his tone annoyed, and just this side of abrasive.

"I can get it," she said, reaching higher. She felt the hem of her top brush the undersides of her breasts.

"Don't," he said. He moved behind her and put his hands on her arms, lowering them to her sides. Then he gently but firmly moved her aside. "You'll strain yourself. I'll get it."

He easily lifted down the ice bucket.

"Thanks," she said, then pulled a bottle of wine from the refrigerator. "Would you like to do the honors?"

He shook his head and a muscle tightened in his jaw. "Actually, I just remembered that there's some work at the office I need to finish." His voice sounded strangled. "Zane was in a hurry to get home to Gwen, and I completely forgot about some figures—" his gaze lowered to her midriff, then went lower to her ankles "—I mean numbers. I have some numbers to work up. Very important," he mumbled as he picked up his briefcase and headed to the lower level of the house where the garage was located. "I just came home for the car. Don't hold dinner. I'm not sure how long this is going to take."

She heard him exit the house, then the car door slam. The automatic garage door went up, then down again after he backed out. Then she heard the sound of a car leaving the drive.

Mattie pulled her casserole from the oven and disgustedly tossed the pot holders on the ceramic tile countertop. "You're not the only chicken who lives here," she said, hearing the catch in her voice.

Feeling like a rejected sixteen-year-old again, Mattie walked over to her romantic table and turned over Dawson's plate. "It takes a special kind of stupid to turn down what I'm offering,'' she said to the empty room.

Then she brushed the single tear from her cheek as she turned off the fire in the hearth. If only the fire inside her could be snuffed out as easily.

"So you want to tell me what happened?'' Mallory Prescott Fortune asked.

Standing beside his sister on the balcony outside his kitchen, Dawson studied her. He sometimes forgot how beautiful she was. Only three inches shorter than his own five foot eleven, she was tall and slender. Her hazel eyes were the same shade as his own, as was her long brown sun-streaked hair. She and her new husband Reed had joined he and Mattie for a goodbye dinner before heading back to Australia. Reed planned to modernize his family's horse operation patterning it after techniques he'd been observing on the Double Crown Ranch. Mallory wanted to use her degree in interior design. While he talked to his sister, Mattie and Reed were in the family room sharing horse stories.

"What happened?'' he said, repeating her question. "Nothing happened.''

That was a bald-faced lie. Since he didn't know how long it would be before he saw his sister again, he didn't want to spoil this visit with anything as disturbing as the truth. Because the truth was that *everything* had happened—all of it bad. His whole life had turned upside down, and he deserved every moment of hell he was going through.

Hellish experience number 1—putting Mattie in a separate bedroom when he wanted her so much that he ached from it. Hellish experience number 2—sharing a wonderful breakfast with her, only to learn that she was going to spend the day with the cowboys on the Double Crown. Jealousy had licked at him until she'd met him at the door that night. She'd made a great dinner and had done the same every night since…setting him up for hellish experience number 3—having to save her from him by turning his back on the romantic evening she'd created. Every nerve in his body had urged him to scoop her into his arms, carry her off to bed and make love to her all night long.

He wasn't sure how long he could share living space with her before making love to her again. If he didn't care about her so much, it wouldn't be a problem. But the last thing he wanted was to hurt her any more than he already had.

"Sell it to someone who's buying, Dawson." Mallory shook her head in disgust. "This is me you're talking to. Something happened all right. Your wedding to Mattie had all the earmarks of a shotgun wedding. I could practically see the imprint of a double-barrel on the back of your tux. How did you and Mattie wind up married?"

He sighed. "Have you ever analyzed the power of guilt?"

"No. But I think I see where you're headed. Do you want to tell it like it is, or should I just use my overactive imagination?"

"I seduced Mattie. She was a virgin. If that isn't bad enough, her brother Griff found us."

"Oh, Lord." Mallory shook her head sympathetically. Then she made a great show of checking him over from head to toe. "No broken bones. I don't recall any black eyes or bruises to spoil the wedding photos. How did Griff convince you to marry Mattie?'' She snapped her fingers. ''Shotgun.''

He laughed. ''If he has one, I never saw it.'' Dawson rested his elbows on the railing and looked out over the pool, the cement deck and the grass area beyond. ''He brought the subject up, but not before I'd come to the same conclusion. Marrying her was the only thing to do. It's my fault that we're in this mess.''

''First of all, I think you need to cut yourself some slack on the seduction issue. Mattie is a tomboy with the heart of a temptress.''

''What's that supposed to mean?'' he asked, not sure whether or not he needed to defend his wife's honor. But the vision of candles, flowers, fireplace and Mattie in an outfit that left him hard and aching flashed through his mind. Definitely a temptress.

''She grew up with five brothers on a ranch. Then she gets a haircut and a makeup lesson, and turns into a raving beauty ready to take that new look out for a spin and see what it can do. What it did was speed up your libido from zero to sixty in the blink of an eye. Bottom line, Dawson—it takes two to tango.''

''That's a cliché.''

''Because it's true. You are not the only one to blame for this.''

''That's what Mattie said as she turned down my first two marriage proposals.''

Mallory smiled as she nodded approvingly. ''I knew I liked her. How did you get her to accept?''

''Actually, Griff did, by invoking the words that strike terror into any kid's heart—what will Mom and Dad say? But if I'd had more self-control, we wouldn't be in this situation.''

"Mattie Fortune—Prescott," she amended, "doesn't strike me as the kind of woman who can be forced to do something she doesn't want to do. Case in point, her wedding ensemble."

Dawson grinned. "She was really something, wasn't she?"

"Yes, and like I said, she has the heart of a temptress. I'd lay odds that her heart is set on you."

"That's where you're wrong," Dawson scoffed. "What would she see in me? I'm just like Dad."

"That makes you a Prescott," Mallory said with a smile. "And you have all of the best Prescott qualities."

"You're biased," he said, returning her smile.

"True. But that's not the point," his sister answered.

"Then what is?"

"You only get one shot at the great love of your life. I think Mattie is yours."

"And why's that?" he asked.

"Because no one can force us Prescotts to do anything we don't want to do. For example, I ran out on my wedding to the man my parents chose because I knew in my heart he wasn't 'the one.' When I met Reed, sparks flew. The same thing happened to you when you met Mattie."

He laughed. "We wanted to strangle each other."

"So did Reed and I. But he was the right one. In a nutshell—don't blow it, bro. You'll regret it."

When she finished her heartfelt speech, Dawson leaned down and kissed her cheek.

"What was that for?" she asked.

"For being such a romantic."

"And smart, too," she said, giving him a hug. "Think about it."

"Will do."

Later, her brother and Reed went to the market while Mattie sat on the couch in the family room, staring thoughtfully into the blazing fire. Her sister-in-law sat cross-legged on the floor beside the hearth, clearly savoring the warmth.

"What's wrong, Mattie?" she asked.

"I forgot about dessert."

"No worries," Mallory said.

"Are you making fun of my accent or do you just like that expression?" Mattie asked with a fleeting grin.

"Both. But truly, don't worry about it. Dawson and Reed will be back in a few minutes with something to satisfy our sweet tooth. I'm sending mental telepathy that it's to be gooey and chocolate."

"I feel so inadequate. What kind of a wife am I?" She bit the corner of her lip, cutting off the threat of a sob slipping out. Her anxiety had nothing to do with chocolate, and everything to do with the fact that she couldn't make Dawson invite her into his bed.

"What is it?" Mallory asked. "This is more than just forgetting dessert. Is it the circumstances of your marriage?"

"You know about that?" Mattie felt her cheeks grow warm, and it certainly wasn't from the fire in the fireplace. Reluctantly, she met her sister-in-law's gaze.

"Dawson told me pretty much everything. He said you tried to take the blame, too, but Griff wouldn't listen."

"My brother is a blockhead. And for a brilliant man, *your* brother is a moron." Mattie realized what she'd said and who she'd said it to. "I'm sorry, Mallory. I didn't mean—"

"Yes, you did," she interrupted. "And when you're right, far be it from me to contradict you. But why do *you* think he's a moron?"

Mattie threw up her hands. "I've tried everything I can think of to make this marriage work."

"Why isn't it working? It's only been a short time. How can you tell?"

"For starters, we aren't sleeping in the same bed. I bet Brody and Jillian don't have that problem. Or you and Reed." Mattie saw the dreamy smile on her sister-in-law's face, and knew she'd spent last night in the arms of the man she loved.

"No, we definitely sleep in the same bed," Mallory said, confirming her suspicions. "But you two are newlyweds. You've already done the wild thing. I don't understand why you—"

"I don't want things to be this way," she assured the other woman. "But I'm afraid to just come out and ask him about it. If he turned me down, I don't know if I could take it—" She bit her lip again.

"Have you tried?"

"Seducing him?" Mattie nodded vigorously. "I fixed a wonderful dinner, set out candles and flowers in front of the fireplace. Got a bottle of wine. Bought a sensational outfit."

"What happened?" Mallory asked.

"He mumbled something about having unfinished work at the office. He couldn't get out of here fast enough. He just doesn't want me."

"I don't believe that for a second. If anything, my guess would be that he's trying to protect you."

"From what?" Mattie asked, bewildered.

"I couldn't say. But Dawson takes care of the people he loves. He married you to protect you. And tonight I've seen the way he looks at you whenever you're in the room. He can't take his eyes off you. Mattie, he's a goner."

"You're just a hopeless romantic," Mattie scoffed. "I don't think I believe in happy endings anymore."

"I'm a hope*ful* romantic. Although I admit your happy ending might take a bit of work." Mallory shifted her position, stretching her legs out as if they were cramped.

"What kind of work?"

"Make him jealous," her sister-in-law suggested. "It worked for me with your brother. When my ex-fiancé showed up here, it got Reed's attention in a big way."

"But I don't have an ex-fiancé. I've never even had another boyfriend. How am I going to make Dawson jealous?"

"You work at the Double Crown, right?"

Mattie nodded. "But the cowboys are my friends. Almost like brothers to me."

"Dawson doesn't know that."

"I have to admit, he didn't seem too happy when I told him one of the cowboys was picking me up and giving me a ride to the ranch," she admitted.

"See?" Mallory said, warming to her subject.

"I don't know," Mattie said, shaking her head doubtfully. "I don't think I can play games like that."

"If my brother is as jealous as I think he is, you won't have to do anything but stand next to another guy."

"I'll think about it," Mattie agreed. "Thanks for listening."

The front door opened and her brother Reed walked in with Dawson right behind him. Mattie's heart beat faster at the sight of her husband. Was Mallory right? Would she get his attention if he thought another man was interested in her?

Reed went directly to his wife and kissed her. Mattie sighed at the appealing picture they made. Her brother's blond hair, pale blue eyes, and rugged good looks were an attractive counterpoint to his wife's femininity.

Dawson set a package on the kitchen table, then joined them in the family room. "So what have you girls been talking about?" he asked, looking from one to the other.

Mallory's eyes took on a mischievous twinkle as she said, "Not much. Just about brothers being block-heads."

Thirteen

Two weeks later, Dawson decided his sister's words definitely fit him to a *T* tonight. He was, indeed, a blockhead.

He'd left the warmth of his house in the suburbs. His suit jacket was forgotten in the car. And now he hunched his shoulders against the bitter December wind as he walked to the barn on the Double Crown. After work, he'd driven to the ranch, poked his head in the house to say a quick hello to Ryan and Lily, then headed back out into the cold. Why?

Mattie.

The answer came to him as clear as the Texas sky above filled with twinkling stars. When she'd called the office and left a message with his secretary that she would be home late, he'd decided to drop by and surprise her. But on the drive out, he'd realized a couple of things.

His reasoning had less to do with a surprise, than it did with the fact that he didn't relish the idea of going home to an empty house. Somehow, Mattie had insinuated herself into his life, and she'd done it without effort in a sinfully short period of time. That big, cold house without her warm, whirlwind presence was as desolate as the Texas prairie on a cloudy night.

The second reason he'd driven out here had a whole lot to do with atonement. Ever since the night he'd run out on her romantic dinner, he'd been haunted by the wounded look in her gray eyes. He hadn't meant to hurt her. In fact, every single thing he did was to keep from doing just that.

"And it's working just great," he muttered sarcastically. The wind howled past his ears in response.

She was young and vulnerable; he was older and wiser. It was up to him to take charge and make sure she didn't get in over her head with a guy like him. If he were a better man, a man worthy of love from a woman like Mattie, things would be different. But he'd proved in spades that he wasn't. All he could do now was minimize battle damage and protect her from himself.

The third reason he'd decided to surprise her was to protect Mattie from other guys who had things on their minds besides transportation to and from the ranch. No way could he convince her not to work on the Double Crown. The horses were too important to her. And she was too good with them. She had a gift, and it would be a crime if she didn't use it. But the thought of the Double Crown ranch hands using their hands on her while chauffeuring her made him nuts. Until he got her a car of her own, he decided, he would taxi her back and forth himself.

He stopped outside the barn and saw light around the door, then heard voices. When he recognized Mattie's, his breath quickened. It had nothing to do with walking uphill; it was the seductive quality wrapped around every word that passed her full, kissable lips that made him hard with need. Next he heard a masculine voice, and his gut clenched. It hadn't occurred to him that she was working with anyone else. Who was in there with her?

The door creaked as he swung it wide, and instantly the scents that assailed him left no doubt that he was in a barn. He looked down the dusty, hay-strewn aisle between gated stalls, spotting Mattie at the end—with a guy he'd never seen before. A cowboy. A *young* cowboy. No doubt about that, what with the hat, boots, denims and work shirt. At this distance he couldn't tell for sure, but he thought the cowboy was just a kid, closer to Mattie's age than his own. The thought made his throat constrict.

He watched her for a moment, coiling a length of rope. Her movements were graceful and confident. She was in her element, her world. When she reached up to hang the lariat on the nail nearby, Dawson's gut tightened another notch. A vision flashed through his mind of her midriff, her flesh bared to his gaze as her top slid up bit by bit, when she stretched for something in his kitchen cupboard. The memory made him long to see even a glimpse of her beautiful breasts. If he'd stayed a second longer that evening, he would have stretched her out on the kitchen table and made love to her right there. Had she known what the sight of her that way did to him? Was she trying to make the young cowboy feel that same gut-twisting need? Like he wanted to scoop her up, lay her out, and love her until neither of them had any strength left? At the thought of another man touching her that way, white-hot fury shot through him.

When she'd replaced the rope, Mattie leaned back against the gate, one leg bent with her boot heel resting on a slat. The cowboy stood across from her, thumbs hooked in his jeans pockets. Neither of them had noticed him yet. If she'd been with anyone besides a cowboy, his blood pressure might have stayed steady.

But he knew that kid was exactly the kind of mate she'd wanted for herself, and Dawson had robbed her of the chance to be with him.

The thought made him angry—mostly at himself. Even though he knew it was wrong, it added insult to injury. All he could think about was getting her away from this guy and having her all to himself.

He started toward them, and his shoes rustled the straw.

She looked up, straightening as he drew closer. "Dawson."

"Mattie."

"You're probably the last person I would have expected to see in the barn," she said, glancing at his dusty black loafers and city-slicker slacks.

Was that a guilty look on her face? He was a couple of feet away and couldn't tell for sure. It could have been pleasure at the sight of him, but he wouldn't bet his last dollar on it. Why would she be glad to see him? She was with a good-looking cowboy. A *young,* good-looking cowboy. Dawson suddenly felt old and tired. Old and just plain old. Followed by more old and really angry. A combustible combination.

"I got your message, that you were working late," he said.

She nodded. "The foreman hired a new hand."

"Yeah. So I noticed." He eyed kid cowboy.

Mattie glanced at her lanky, dark-haired, blue-eyed companion. "This is Zach Conroy. All the other guys had errands in town. I offered to show him the ropes."

"Literally?" Dawson asked, glancing at the rope she had just hung up.

She chuckled. "No pun intended."

Zach stuck his hand out. "Nice to meet you, sir."

Dawson winced at the word *sir,* a term of respect he'd always given his father. Since Dawson had turned into a Geoffrey Prescott clone, he figured ''sir'' was probably appropriate. But having the word directed at him was like having salt rubbed in a festering wound.

He contemplated ignoring the kid's hand, but couldn't forget that he was also his mother's son, taught to mind his manners. ''Welcome to the Double Crown, Zach. You couldn't have a better teacher than my *wife.*''

''No, sir.'' The kid slid him a nervous look.

''My *husband* is a shameless flatterer.'' Mattie mimicked his emphasis, but she looked at him as if he'd grown another head.

''It's not flattery if it's the truth,'' he countered.

''Dawson, what are you doing all the way out here?'' she asked, her tone reflecting confusion that was just this side of exasperation.

Protecting you from the likes of him, he thought. Instead he said, ''I'm here to give you a lift home.''

She smiled warmly as if his explanation pleased her. ''What a nice surprise. Shall I ask Aunt Lily if we can stay for supper. It's late and—''

He shot Zach a withering glance, then took her arm and started walking toward the door. ''Mattie's off duty. You're on your own, kid,'' he said to the cowboy. In a lower voice he said to her, ''It is late. I want to get you home.''

Get you home.

The words sang through Mattie's mind all the way to the house. They were just dripping with suggestion. What would he do with her when he got her home? She dearly hoped that it would be more than when he'd gotten her home on their wedding night. She fervently prayed it would be a lot more than her dismal failure of a romantic dinner. Maybe his feelings were changing. He certainly hadn't acted like himself when he'd found her in the barn with Zach.

Was he jealous? Was Mallory right about his showing his affection if he thought she was interested in someone else? There was unmistakable strain in him. He'd hardly said two words all the way home. He'd driven as if he couldn't leave the ranch behind fast enough. And his pace never slowed as they set a land-speed record on the highway back to the house. Her body hummed with anticipation, and her heart soared with hope that he would love her, body and soul.

He braked the car in front of the garage and pressed the door opener. Mattie opened her mouth to say something, then glanced at Dawson. Tension hardened his features and tightened his mouth to a straight line. His shoulders were rigid and his knuckles white as he gripped the steering wheel.

She closed her mouth. It could wait.

They entered the kitchen, and Mattie suddenly felt grungy from her day's work. "I'm going to take a shower," she said.

"Suit yourself."

Not the response of a man intent on ravishing his woman, she thought as doubt crept in. She went into her room and stripped off her boots, jeans, shirt and undergarments. In the shower, she washed her hair as she puzzled over Dawson. He was annoyed with her, and she wasn't exactly sure why. It had something to do with Zach. But Zach was just a kid. The more she puzzled, the more uneasy she became. Her neck muscles tightened and she realized Dawson's tension was contagious. Damn him, anyway. She always looked forward to her evening shower. Thanks to him and his little tizzy, she couldn't even enjoy it. Maybe it was time to get things out in the open between them.

She shut the water off, then grabbed a big, fluffy bath towel and wrapped it around herself. In her dressing area, she took another towel and dried her hair, before running a comb through it. When she walked into her bedroom, she saw Dawson standing beside the bed. She had the feeling that he'd paced like a caged beast while she'd showered. His eyes had the look of a hungry tiger ready to do battle for his primal needs. She clutched her towel, then realized she wasn't exactly dressed for battle. Or was she?

"If you're through, I have a few things to say to you." He planted his feet wide apart. Then, almost unwillingly, his gaze lowered from her eyes to the knot where her towel came together over her breasts. His eyes narrowed and his nostrils flared slightly as if he were scenting his prey. "Put some clothes on first."

"Just say what you have to say." She might not have her armor on, but she wasn't going to back down from a confrontation. She lowered her hands to her sides and lifted her chin. "Fire when ready," she said.

"Your call," he said with a shrug. But his hands were a little unsteady as he stuck them in his pockets. "For starters—you and Zach alone in the barn."

Aha! She'd been right. At least he didn't beat around the bush. "I already told you. I offered to show him the ranch. In your line of work I believe you call it 'orientation.'"

"And just what else were you *orienting* him about?" he asked, his eyes narrowing on her. "The two of you looked mighty cozy."

"I resent your tone and that question. We were merely talking."

"I didn't like it."

"He's new. He doesn't know anyone. We were just getting acquainted."

"I still didn't like it."

"Why not? What in the world was there to object to? Talking in the barn?"

"Maybe the fact that nine out of ten guys talking to a beautiful woman in the barn would want a roll in the hay."

Her temper snapped. "Apparently I married number ten, the only man who doesn't want me—in the barn, in his bed, or anywhere else for that matter."

"Shows how much you know about men," he muttered. His gaze raked over her—from her bare feet and legs, over her abdomen, to her breasts. A muscle in his jaw contracted, and his eyes darkened. "Where's your common sense, Mattie? You don't know that guy."

"No. But all my instincts tell me he's a good guy."

"You're a sitting duck all alone in the barn. What if your instincts were wrong?"

She hoped to God they were right, because her instincts were commanding her to do something now, that could send her to heaven—or land her in hell. She was going to put everything on the line—her body, her heart, her soul.

Mattie dropped her towel. "My mother once said that arguing naked was the prescription for a healthy marriage." But she was so scared that he would turn his back on her. Then what would she do?

He swallowed hard as his eyes devoured her. "Only

one of us is naked,'' he said in a hoarse voice, as one corner of his mouth quirked.

At least he'd stopped yelling at her about being alone in the barn. But that wasn't all. The bulge in his slacks told her that he wanted her.

Mattie's heart started to pound when he moved toward her. He reached out a trembling hand and cupped her face in his palm. It was the only sign she needed. She started to unbutton his shirt. He ripped it from his waistband, then helped her with the buttons before dragging it off his shoulders. Her breath caught at the sight of his bare chest, its masculine sprinkling of hair tapering down to disappear into his trousers.

As if he knew what she was thinking, he unbuckled his belt and undid the hook on his pants. The bulge there made her heart and spirit soar with the knowledge of her power.

Then he met her gaze. She knew he was giving her the opportunity to refuse to go any further. This was the point of no return.

She reached out and rested her hand over his heart, and felt it pound. ''One of us still has too many clothes on,'' she said, her tone husky.

He sucked in a breath. ''I'm luckier than nine out of ten guys. And you're mistaken about me not wanting you.''

''I've never been happier to be wrong,'' she whispered, her heart so full that she didn't trust her voice.

His eyes darkened even more, and in the next instant Dawson gripped her arms just short of hurting her. He lowered his mouth to hers in a crushing kiss. Her heart beat so hard that it nearly flew from her chest as her breathing escalated. In spite of his words, she felt the anger and passion warring within him. She had no idea what demons he struggled against. But for now, it was just her and Dawson and if there was any justice in the world, she would make him forget everything but her.

Mattie opened her mouth to him, inviting him inside. When his tongue invaded, she touched it with the tip of her own, and smiled with satisfaction when his breathing grew more ragged. She felt his desperation, his urgency, as he backed away long enough to tear off the rest of his clothes. Then she was in his arms, skin to skin, soft to hard, woman to man.

He backed her up until she felt the bed behind her. The next thing she knew, she was on her back with Dawson above her. He spread her legs apart with his knee, and she willingly obliged. With a gentleness that belied the fierce expression on his face, he touched her most intimate femininity. As he inserted a finger, she felt herself throbbing; she closed around him, welcoming this imitation of the intimacy she craved.

"You're so ready," he said in a strangled voice.

Shocked at her boldness, yet trusting her instincts, she took his manhood in her hand. He sucked in a breath and trembled. "So are you," she murmured.

She stroked his shaft and marveled at the silky softness. Moving her hand slowly, tenderly, she explored him.

He gasped and put his hand over hers. "Stop."

"Why?"

"If you don't, in about ten seconds it will be all over." He closed his eyes and shuddered. There was a fierce look of concentration on his face. When he opened his eyes, he said, "Besides, I don't want to hurt you."

"How can this hurt me? You don't need to protect

me. Not from this. I want you. I've wanted you ever since that first time. Don't you get it? Just love me—''

"Damn it, Mattie." His voice was nearly a growl. "You don't know what you're saying."

"Yes, I do. You can roar at me all you want. But I am woman—I'll roar right back."

Despite his words, he continued to stroke her. As bolts of desire zapped her, she found it increasingly difficult to think straight. To make a rational argument about why it was all right to continue doing what they were doing. It was time to just do it. Still holding him in her hand, she positioned him at the opening of her womanhood. She smiled to herself when he groaned.

"I have to be inside you."

"Yes. Please. Now," she cried.

He entered her fast and hard, and she gloried in his possession. She had never felt more feminine, more womanly than she did at this moment. There was no pain this time, just pure physical satisfaction and intense pleasure that flowed through her like liquid fire. Oh, she was warm. Every part of her was hot.

He leaned forward to kiss her, and at the same time took most of his weight on his elbows. She lifted her hips, thrusting against him.

"Easy, Mattie. Slow and easy does it." Dawson brushed the hair back from her face and gently kissed her forehead, nose, jaw, and a spot just beneath her ear that nearly sent her to the great beyond. "I've wanted you, too, ever since the first time. I'm not sure I can hold out."

"We've got all night," she said, frustrated. She'd waited, too, and she was *ready*.

"Yes." But he continued to kiss her face slowly, sweetly.

She throbbed with need and started a slow, subtle, sexy hip rhythm. "Please, Dawson."

He groaned again. "Mattie, stop."

"Please, Dawson," she said, sensing his imminent surrender.

"Not yet."

She wiggled against him and heard his sharp intake of breath. "Witch," he growled. "If that's the way you want it."

"It is," she answered.

"You asked for it."

He moved against her, and she received him as he thrust again and again. In the center of her belly, a knot tightened. With each lunge she felt herself moving closer and closer to the breaking point. She wrapped her legs around him, and this time his rasping breath seemed to come from deep in his soul.

"Oh, Mattie. That feels so good."

"I'm glad," she whispered, placing her palms on his chest. She brushed the pads of her thumbs across his nipples and felt them tighten.

With every thrust, the pressure inside her built, until she silently begged for release. Finally, there was a jolt of electricity where their bodies joined that created an explosion of bright light behind her eyes. Tremors shook her body. His arms shaking with tension, Dawson held her until she went still. Then he lunged once more and stopped. Her eyes opened in time to see a fierce look on his face. He made a sound deep in his throat, then he gathered her to his chest as he claimed his own release.

He rolled to his side. Still holding her in his arms, he carried her with him and snuggled her against him.

His chest expanded from the huge breath he took in. "So," he said.

"So," she answered.

"How do you feel?"

Good question. Warm fuzzys. Glowing. Content. Happy. The feelings were so big, so deep, so wonderful, she didn't have the words to express the delicious sensation. So she simply said, "I love you."

Fourteen

Dawson straightened his tie as he walked down the hall to the kitchen. The smells of breakfast drifted to him and his mouth started to water, not so much at the thought of food, but at the thought of the cook. *Mattie.* How had she so quickly become part of his life?

Waking up with her in his arms just a short time ago was the best thing that had ever happened to him. Her silky hair had spilled over his shoulders and trickled down his chest, teasing him with erotic promise. He had never seen a more beautiful sight than a drowsy Mattie, blinking sleep from her eyes, then her radiant smile when she'd noticed that he was watching her. Followed again by the words that still shook him to his soul.

I love you.

The happiness in her expression slipped a little when he hadn't responded in kind; he had just kissed the tip of her cute little nose. But he just couldn't say what she wanted to hear. And yet, he couldn't let it just hang there between them. A dialogue over breakfast was just what they needed to clear the air.

He walked into the kitchen and stopped in the doorway to watch her butter toast. Dressed in a T-shirt tucked into jeans that hugged her hips and legs, she made even that mundane chore seem sexy. Knowing he would hate himself later, he walked up behind her and put his hands at her waist, then nuzzled her neck.

"Mmm," she said dreamily, tipping her head to the side to give him better access. "Good morning."

"How did you sleep?" he asked, hoping her rest had been better than his own.

"Like a rock." She turned into him and automatically wrapped her arms around his waist as she nestled into his chest.

He told himself that it was wrong to pull her against him. He also knew after last night that he could never go back to not touching her at all.

She lifted her lips to his for a sweet, almost chaste kiss that left him wanting to turn up the heat, to get out of the kitchen and back to the bedroom. But this wasn't the time or place.

Apparently she felt the same, because she patted his tie and stepped back. "How do you want your eggs this morning?"

"Scrambled." Like his mind.

"Okay." She turned back to the stove and cracked some eggs into a bowl, then beat them with a whisk.

His gaze dropped to her shapely derriere, then lower to her legs. He remembered the feel of them wrapped around his waist just a few hours earlier. The reality of her gesture, drawing him deeper inside her, was even more wonderfully erotic than the fantasies he'd had since first laying eyes on her. He grew hard at the thought, and shifted uncomfortably. This line of thinking wouldn't get him anywhere.

She divided the cooked eggs onto two plates, added bacon, fried potatoes and toast, then set them on the table. "Coffee?" she asked.

"I'll get it." He poured himself a mug, then sat

down at the table across from her. *Here goes nothing,* he thought. "About last night—" He stopped as a sweet, contented smile turned up the corners of her full mouth.

She looked like a woman completely fulfilled by her husband. That was good news—and bad. Good because she'd taken to the marriage bed like a duck to water. He couldn't help being glad that he'd satisfied her so completely that she wouldn't look to another man—especially a cowboy—for fulfillment. And he had never experienced with any woman the satisfaction he had with Mattie last night.

But bad because there was more to this than just the physical. Her emotional needs were much more complicated. And so important.

"What about last night?" she asked. "If you need to lodge a protest, the complaint department is now open."

"I would be a fool to complain about a night like we had." Her saucy grin made him throb with need. "But we have to talk about what you said."

"What? When?" She took a bite of toast as her smooth forehead creased with a frown.

She'd said it several more times. The words came so naturally to her that he wasn't surprised she didn't have a clue what he was talking about. Coming from a big, loving family, affection had been a constant in her life. It was something taken for granted. He envied her; he hadn't been so lucky. His father hadn't been around much, and his mother had needed *his* emotional support after the divorce. She'd been in no condition to nurture.

"When I asked how you felt after we made love."

"Which time?" she asked, grinning wickedly.

"The first time," he said, exasperated because it was difficult to stay focused with her. Damn, she was distracting. He had to agree with her mother about naked arguing. It was sure to end any disagreement. "And I was talking about physically. But you said—"

"I love you," she interrupted.

"Right." He rested his forearms on the table and met her gaze. "I know you want me to say it back."

She stared at him for several moments, then shook her head and frowned. "I don't think I want to talk about this now."

Dawson squarely met her gaze. "Waiting won't make the problem disappear, Mattie."

"I never said it would. I just don't think this is a good time."

"It's as good a time as any. I believe in honesty and communication." *Unlike my father,* he thought. If his old man had just been honest with his mother, their whole sordid mess would have been easier to deal with.

"Honesty and communication are good. At a mutually convenient time."

"I'll make this quick. You said you loved me."

She nodded. "And I meant it."

He wanted to ask her why. He had taken her virginity and spoiled her for another man. He'd used her badly and forced her into marriage because of it. She had forfeited her hopes and dreams because of his baser needs. He couldn't believe that what she felt for him was love.

"I care about you—a lot," he said. "But I can't say that I love you." He winced as the light in her eyes seemed to flicker.

She looked as if he'd just hit her, and he felt lower

than a snake's belly. Then she lifted her chin and met his gaze. He couldn't help admiring her guts. She was a hell of a woman.

"I never asked you to," she said.

"But you want to hear the words."

"Every woman wants that," she said. "But not if you don't mean it."

"I care about you more than I've cared for any woman, Mattie."

She shook her head. "Don't lie to me, Dawson."

"It's not a lie. That's not my style."

She nodded, satisfied. "Good. I'll hold you to that and believe you care. It's a start. Love has grown under weirder circumstances."

He ran a hand through his hair. "That's just it, Mattie. I don't know what love is. I'm uncomfortable with the word."

"Okay. You don't have to say it. Just don't expect me to *not* say it."

"Can't we leave love out of this? We have something better."

"Better?" She looked incredulous. "What could possibly be better than love?"

He saw the look in her eyes and knew he'd made a serious error. He'd forgotten that this was the same woman who'd fantasized about a marriage proposal complete with candlelight dinner and her intended on one knee when he popped the question. She was a hopeless romantic dressed in denim instead of lace. The funny part was, he wouldn't have her any other way. Did that mean he loved her? He didn't know.

"I'll tell you what's better than love. Respect," he said, nodding emphatically.

"Respect?" She looked even more incredulous. In

fact, she looked like she might be contemplating slugging him.

He nodded. "I have learned to regard you with admiration and affection."

"If you can't love me, Dawson, at least have the guts to just say so. Don't throw twenty-dollar words at me and think that makes everything a-okay."

"That's not—"

"Don't interrupt. If you can't really care about me, don't tippy-toe around the issue and cover it up. Say it straight out."

There was a *honk* from outside.

"What's that?" he asked.

"My ride," she said, pushing her practically untouched plate of food away. She stood.

"I'm taking you to the ranch."

"Since when?"

Since last night. But apparently he'd forgotten to mention it to her. "I'll go out and tell whichever of your cowboy chauffeurs is waiting that I'm driving you in later."

She shook her head. "I'd rather ride with the devil himself. You can take your respect and stick it—" She stopped and took a deep breath. Her voice was sad when she said, "I'm going to work now. I hope you and your respect have a wonderful day." She half turned, then rounded on him again. "And I hope that respect warms your bed tonight."

Then she turned on her heel and walked out. Dawson started to follow, but the phone rang. He looked at it, then at Mattie's retreating back. He wanted to go after her, but couldn't ignore the insistent ringing. It could be news about Clint Lockhart. Until the man was caught, he wouldn't breathe easier about Mattie's safety. As much as he hated the idea of her riding to work with one of the ranch hands, it was better than her going by herself.

As he picked up the phone, he heard the front door slam, and flinched as the windows rattled. "Hello?"

"When did you plan to tell me that I have a daughter-in-law?" asked the familiar female voice.

"Hello, Mother." Dawson sighed as he took the remote receiver and sat in Mattie's chair. "How are you?"

"Fine. Actually, that's not entirely accurate. I'm miffed that you didn't see fit to let me know that you were married."

"How did you find out?"

There was a chuckle on the other end of the line. "So you're only sorry that you got caught."

"Yes, and that I haven't had a chance to fill you in. How did you find out?" he asked again.

"Mallory told her mother, who told a mutual friend, who mentioned it thinking I already knew." She tsked. "I nearly choked. A heck of a way to find out your only son is married."

So he'd screwed up. What else was new?

"Sorry, Mother. I'm not going to bore you with excuses."

"Are you even going to tell me her name?"

"Matilda—Mattie Fortune. She's from the Australian branch of the family."

"Tell me everything. And start with the excuses. I have a feeling they're the juicy part."

He picked up Mattie's fork and pushed eggs around her plate. "It was a whirlwind affair, and we got caught up in a double wedding ceremony with Mattie's brother Brody. I knew you were traveling and wouldn't be able to get back in time. Reed and Mallory are on their way to live in Australia, and we all wanted to get married while they were still here.'' He looked at the door his wife had slammed only moments before. ''And life with Mattie is never dull.''

''What's wrong, Dawson?''

He could almost hear a frown in his mother's voice. ''Nothing.''

Everything. His answer was automatic as it always was with his mother. He'd taken on the role of her protector and old habits died hard. But he couldn't help wondering how women were able to read him so well. Especially his mother. He was always the one trying to cheer her up. Get her over the depression and resentment of being dumped for a younger woman. Somewhere in all that, the dynamics of their relationship had shifted. He'd always felt like the parent, and she the child. He didn't think she knew him at all.

''Don't give me that 'nothing' garbage, son. I know I haven't always been there for you when you needed me. I apologize for that. But I'm here now. And I can hear in your voice that you're upset about something. Tell me what's really going on. What's bothering you?''

He'd told Mallory. What harm could it do to let his mother in on the sordid details? ''I married Mattie because I seduced her.''

There was a noise on the other end of the phone that sounded an awful lot like a snort. His mother never snorted.

''That happens all the time,'' she said. ''And men don't feel obligated to marry the woman.'' There was a pause. ''Is she pregnant?''

He hoped not. ''No. But she was a virgin.''

Another snort. "Pregnancy and virginity aren't mutually exclusive, Dawson. Your father, the doctor, was supposed to have explained all this to you twenty years ago."

He laughed. "He did. I know all about the birds and bees."

"Good." There was another pause on the line, then she said, "You know, son, you're a lot like him."

"Now there's a recommendation," he said wryly.

"You have no reason to believe me after all the disparaging remarks you heard about your father over the years. But he was a good man. Just like you."

Now it was his turn to snort. "Yeah. Hold on while I dust off my wings and halo." He heard her laughter.

"He was also flawed, just like you." She sighed. "Dawson, I'm a selfish woman. I've struggled with it all my life. It cost me your father, and I withdrew from you. He and I ran out of time to rectify the mistake. I won't let the same thing happen with you."

"What are you saying, Mother?"

"Your father and I started having problems because I demanded more and more of his time. He was a gifted heart surgeon who had an obligation to use his talent for saving lives. Selfishly, childishly, I asked him for more time than he had to give me. We quarreled constantly, and eventually he turned to someone else for solace and companionship. Probably sex, too."

"What's your point? I'm sure you have one, Mother."

"You bet I do. He came to me once after he'd married again. He asked what I thought about a reconciliation."

"What happened?" He knew his shock at her revelation was evident in his voice.

"I turned him down." Her voice caught, and she was silent for several moments. But emotion crackled through the phone line. Finally she said, "It was the second stupidest thing I've ever done in my life."

"What was the first?"

"Pushing him away with my constant demands." She sighed. "Dawson, he came to *me*. He admitted that he'd had a midlife crisis and took all the blame. He said that I was the great love of his life. But my pride wouldn't let me forgive him."

"Again, I have to ask what your point is, Mother."

"I hear something in your voice when you talk about Mattie. You've never sounded that way before when telling me about the women in your life. I suspect she's the one."

"The one?"

"Don't be dense, dear. The great love of *your* life. My neediness robbed you of your childhood. I won't let the lessons of my behavior cheat you out of the happiness you deserve. Make it work with Mattie. Bare your soul. Get in touch with your feminine side."

"I don't have one." He chuckled. "You've been taking psychology courses again, haven't you?"

"Yes, but that's beside the point. If your father was right, and I think he was, we only get one good shot at love. He and I had it and were too stupid to hold on to it. Don't repeat our mistake. Don't be like me. Don't miss out on life because of stupid, stubborn, senseless pride. Do as I say, not as I did."

Dawson rubbed his thumb over the tines of Mattie's fork, which he still held. "She told me she loves me.

The first words out of her mouth when she woke up this morning.''

''I hope you responded in kind,'' his mother said.

''Actually, I told her we had something better than love. Respect.''

''Dawson Geoffrey Prescott. I can't believe I raised such a dunderhead.'' She sighed again. ''We reap what we sow. Unfortunately, I sowed some seeds that made you far too cautious. I assume all the blame for your being relationship-impaired. Not to mention spontaneity-challenged.''

''Is that the diagnostic term for it now?''

''Sarcasm is so unattractive, dear. But it's my fault that you've messed up so badly. Maybe I can help. Put Mattie on the phone.''

''She's not here. She trains horses at the Double Crown, and she left a little while ago.''

''Then go after her, Dawson. Tell her what's in your heart.''

''I don't know, Mother—''

''Do it, son,'' she said. There was a thread of steel in her voice that he'd never heard before. ''I let pride and hurt tarnish all the good times your father and I had. Pushing him away condemned me to a life of loneliness without the only man I will ever love. Don't make the same mistake, Dawson.''

''I'll talk to her.''

''Good,'' she said firmly. ''I'm looking forward to meeting Mattie.'' She stopped for a moment, and he could almost hear her thinking. ''One more thing, Dawson.''

''Yes?''

"I love you."

That startled him. She didn't say that often. Neither did he. He hesitated for a few moments before answering truthfully, "I love you, too, Mother."

Fifteen

It was midmorning when Mattie found Lily Fortune in the great room at the Double Crown. She'd been unable to make any progress with the problem horse she'd been given to train. Her concentration was non-existent. Thanks to Dawson. Respect, indeed! How dare he insult her intelligence. At least her gut instinct told her he had. But what did she know about men?

How she longed for her mother to talk to, but she couldn't upset her family with a long-distance phone call. The next best thing was her aunt.

"Can I talk to you for a minute, Aunt Lily?"

The older woman turned. "Of course." She stood in front of the great room fireplace with garland in her hand. A Christmas tree, already decorated, graced a corner of the room. "I could use a break. Would you like a cup of coffee or tea?"

"No, thanks." Mattie shook her head. The thought of coffee turned her stomach. Usually she had a cast-iron constitution. Since she'd never experienced love before, she figured the queasiness was the way her body reacted to man trouble.

"What can I do for you?" Lily asked.

"If you were my fairy godmother, you could turn my frog into a prince," she said, trying to joke. She sat down on the leather couch facing the fireplace.

Lily walked around the coffee table and took a seat beside her. "What's wrong, dear?"

Mattie met the older woman's sympathetic gaze. "Since I was a little girl, all I've ever wanted was to love and be loved. And have a baby."

"That's what most women want. You've taken the first steps to make that happen. You and Dawson found each other and fell in love."

"That's just it," she said, twisting her fingers together. "We found each other, sort of. But we didn't exactly fall in love," she added, remembering his words that morning. Her heart wrenched with sadness.

"I've seen the way you look at him, dear. If it's not love, then I don't know what is."

"It's not me. It's him. He has this whacked-out sense of honor, and it's messed everything up. He makes my body hum, then breaks my heart. He talks about the 'right' thing, but it all feels so wrong." She felt a wave of tears cresting, and covered her face with her hands.

The couch dipped as the other woman slid beside her and put an arm around her shoulders. "Tell me everything."

That was all she needed to hear. Mattie lowered her hands and looked at her aunt. She told her everything that had happened to make her so miserable.

"And why did you agree to the marriage?" Lily asked after listening intently. "Given your attire at the wedding, I have a feeling no one could force you, or Dawson either for that matter, to do anything you truly didn't want to do."

Mattie sighed. "At the time, I thought it was because Griff threatened to go to my folks with the story. Now I realize that I'm in love with Dawson."

"So what's the problem?"

"He doesn't love me back."

"Are you sure about that?" Lily reached out and tucked a strand of Mattie's hair behind her ear. "I've seen the way he looks at you, too. It's not the expression of a man who has no feelings for you."

"Oh, he's got feelings, all right. Something better than love," Mattie said bitterly. "R-E-S-P-E-C-T."

"Did he tell you that?" Lily asked, astounded.

Mattie nodded. "This morning. In bed. After the most wonderful night I've ever—" Her voice broke, and she bit her lip to hold back the sobs.

"Blockhead," Lily mumbled, tightening her arm around Mattie.

"Exactly." Mattie sniffed. "So, I've been thinking, and I've come up with a plan."

"What?"

"I'll stay with Dawson a decent length of time to spare my parents the embarrassment of knowing what really happened between us. Then we'll split up and tell everyone it just didn't work out."

"Mattie, sweetheart, don't rush into a decision like that. It's only been three weeks since the wedding. You need to give the relationship time to grow. Unless I miss my guess, Dawson Prescott is very much in love with you. All this respect nonsense is a smoke screen. He's afraid to say the words."

"But why?"

Lily shrugged. "I don't know all the history. But I think it has a lot to do with his parents' breakup."

"Silly Aunt Lily," Mattie said fondly as she shook her head. "Thanks for trying to spare my feelings. And don't take this the wrong way, but I think you're mistaken. Dawson isn't afraid of anything. If he loved me, he would say so.''

''Sweetie, you grew up with five brothers, but you don't know squat about men. No offense. The men in this family, including Dawson, could face down a grizzly, go nose to snout with an alligator, wrestle a mountain lion to the death for the ones they love. But saying that one small four-letter word scares the hell out of them.''

''Aunt Lily!'' Mattie exclaimed in mock outrage. She grinned, and the other woman smiled in response.

''Just give it some serious thought before you do anything you'll regret,'' Lily said.

''I will.'' Mattie leaned over and kissed her cheek. ''Thanks. You're a terrific stand-in mom.''

''You're welcome.'' Lily hugged her. ''Anytime. And just you leave everything to me.''

''Leave everything to me,'' Mattie mumbled.

''What?'' Dawson asked, glancing at her momentarily, then back to the winding road he drove.

''Nothing. Just talking to myself.'' *For practice,* she added silently. Because she planned never to talk to anyone ever again. Her last bare-her-soul, heart-to-heart chat with her aunt had resulted in Ryan and Lily's thinly veiled plan to save her marriage.

Because of that conversation, Mattie now found herself sitting in Dawson's BMW on the way to the Fortune family cabin near a lake. It belonged to a friend of Lily's. Because of the threat Clint Lockhart presented, Ryan was concerned about sending them to the family cabin. He was afraid the deranged man might know about it. If Mattie had known the words ''Leave everything to me'' meant that her aunt and uncle would give her and Dawson a surprise honeymoon, she might have thought twice about spilling her guts to the older woman.

Last evening, Dawson had come to the Double Crown because he'd said he was worried when she didn't come home on time. Hah! Worry about someone you merely *respected?*

But Ryan and Lily had sat the two of them down and said that since they'd married so quickly and hadn't planned a honeymoon, they were to take it now. Ryan gave Dawson an executive order to take some time off, and insisted Mattie have a vacation from her work on the ranch. They were not to show their faces for at least a week.

And now they were stuck with each other. Alone.

"I think we're there," Dawson said.

He pulled the car into a drive and stopped beside a single-story wooden cabin. Through a thicket of leafless trees, Mattie saw the blue water of the lake.

They got out of the car and unloaded the suitcases from the trunk. Dawson had the cabin key and let them inside where they explored the fully appointed kitchen, living room with stone fireplace on one wall, and four bedrooms. It wasn't fancy compared to the Double Crown, but it was cozy and comfortable.

And far too isolated, Mattie thought. Not a computer or calculator, or horse and saddle in sight. Nothing to distract them or take the heat off.

But heat wasn't their problem. That's what had landed them here in the first place.

She noticed that Dawson put all their luggage in the same bedroom. Was that a good sign? She couldn't afford to let herself hope.

When they'd unpacked clothes and a week's worth

of groceries, they stood on opposite sides of the center island in the kitchen and stared at each other for a few moments.

"Now what?" she asked.

"Talk," he answered. "A person would have to be deaf, dumb and blind to miss what Ryan and Lily are doing."

"Marriage counselors," she answered.

He nodded. "Along with my mother."

"Your mother?"

"Yeah. Contrary to the rumor about me being discovered under a cabbage leaf, I actually have a mother. She called yesterday morning. Right after you left," he added. "She found out about our wedding."

"Is she upset?"

He shook his head. "She pretended to be miffed, but I'd have to say she sincerely wished us every happiness."

"We might be able to be happy. If we get a divorce," she said grimly.

"What?" he looked genuinely shocked.

"Obviously this marriage was a mistake."

"Obvious to whom?" he asked.

"I don't mean to sound ungrateful." She took a deep breath to ward off the pain of the heart-breaking proposal she was about to make. Quite different from the one she'd always dreamed of having from a man. "I think we should wait a decent interval and then separate. We'll tell everyone that it just didn't work out. The rest of the details are easy. I don't want anything. I'm just as responsible for this situation as you are. And I sincerely appreciate what you tried to do. But it just seems wrong for both of us to be unhappy for the rest of our lives."

"This is because I told you I respect you. Because I didn't say I love you." His shocked expression gave way to something that closely resembled anger. "That was stupid. But you have to understand something, Mattie."

"What?" she asked.

"I didn't grow up like you with a normal, loving couple for role models. My father left my mother for a much younger woman when I was ten. It was devastating for her, especially because she felt the age factor left her no weapons to fight with. From then until I left for college, I had my work cut out for me trying to undo the damage my father had done to my mother's self-esteem."

"I'm sorry, Dawson. It must have been horrible for you both to go through that. But I don't see—"

He held up a hand. "I'm not finished yet. All these years I blamed my father for using her, then walking out when he found a younger woman. But my mother told me yesterday that she bears some responsibility, too. She resented the hours he devoted to his patients, his being on call, his long office hours. She demanded more time than he had to give her. She constantly threw in his face that there wasn't enough of him left over for his family."

"I'm so sorry you had to deal with all that."

"I don't want your pity," he said angrily. "I'm just trying to explain that I don't know a lot about relationships. All I learned is that it's not easy to make it work when the people involved are so different. They suffer. And not just the ones *in* the relationship. It's the people around them. Kids."

"What are you trying to say, Dawson?"

He ran a hand through his hair. "I guess I'm trying

to say that two mismatched people have the deck
stacked against them.''

Mattie felt as if he'd just stabbed her through the
heart. Cupid would be hard-pressed to find a man and
woman more mismatched than the two of them. The
miserable look in his eyes confirmed her suspicions.
He agreed that they should separate. Until that moment, she hadn't realized how much she'd wanted him
to talk her out of her divorce idea. Or how deeply
she'd hoped voicing it would shake him up and make
him realize that he *did* love her.

But he agreed with her. The pain of losing Dawson,
of losing the man she loved, settled around her heart
like a stone. It took her breath away. Before she made
a fool of herself in front of him, she needed to be alone
to compose herself.

She turned away from him and headed for the front
door.

''Where are you going?'' he asked. His tone
smacked of surprise or annoyance, or both.

She didn't have the energy to care. ''I need some
air. Please don't follow me. I'd like to be by myself.''

She walked outside and slammed the door behind
her. The December wind made her cheeks tingle. For
a few seconds she focused on that, rather than the fact
that her heart was breaking. She knew there would
never be anyone for her but Dawson. Her mother was
a one-man woman, and Mattie had no doubt it was
the same for her. How could she go on without him?

She saw a trail through the woods and started walking. Her pace was brutal, probably because she was
trying to leave her demons behind. But as tears started
to trickle down her cheeks, she knew she would never
be able to outrun the pain of living without Dawson.

She brushed the moisture from her cheeks, trying to clear her vision and focus on the path in front of her.

The sound of a twig snapping behind her made her stop. Had Dawson ignored her request? Was he following? Foolishly she hoped that was the case, and waited for him to catch up. As she stood in front of a tree, she struggled to catch her breath. Suddenly a wave of dizziness swept over her, followed by a disorienting light-headedness. Blackness closed in, eating up the light. Her body felt heavy, and she felt herself falling.

At the same time, from a great distance, she heard an explosion. Then nothing.

Pacing the cabin like a caged tiger, Dawson heard what sounded like a car backfiring. Not likely, since this area around the lake was way too isolated for other vehicles. A hunter? The noise he'd heard didn't sound like a rifle. Could it have been a pistol shot? *Clint Lockhart?* That threat had been on his mind ever since the day he'd married Mattie and—

Another loud explosion rang out.

''Mattie?'' he whispered.

Fear was a vise squeezing his chest as he raced from the cabin. Ryan had charged him with Mattie's safety, and he'd let him down. More importantly, he'd screwed up what he'd vowed to do. He'd left the woman he loved unprotected. He stopped and frantically looked around, cursing himself for not going with her. Which way had she gone?

''Mattie?'' he called as loudly as he could. The echo of his own voice was the only response.

He saw the path leading into the woods and hoped to God it was the right way. He ran as if the hounds of hell were after him. His footsteps, pounding in the dry leaves on the hard ground, echoed the prayer that played over and over in his head. *Let her be all right.*

Although it seemed a lifetime, only several minutes passed before he saw her—collapsed on the ground at the base of a tree. Not moving. *Oh, God, please don't take her from me.*

He skidded to a stop, then went down on one knee beside her still form. With the threat of more gunfire, he couldn't stay out in the open. He scooped her into his arms and hunched his body around hers, trying to protect her as best he could. He ran with her a short way to a shallow ravine lined with rocks. He ducked behind them and slid the short way down the embankment, cradling her against him. His heavy breathing was the only sound he heard as he waited for more shots.

A few seconds later, he heard the snapping of twigs and the crackle of dead leaves. Someone was running through the trees. As the noise grew more faint, he realized whoever it was—Clint Lockhart, no doubt—was moving away from them. Then he heard nothing but silence and the occasional calling of a bird.

"Mattie?" Still holding her, he brushed silky blond hair back from her face as he scanned her from head to toe. Other than a nasty scrape on her cheek and a bump on her temple, he saw no blood or other sign of trauma. No gunshot wound. Her chest rose and fell, telling him that she was breathing. He sighed with relief.

He ran his hand over her arms and legs in a cursory examination. "Mattie? Sweetheart? Please wake up."

He heard the desperation in his own voice, and asked any god who would listen to an insensitive mo-

ron like himself to bring her back to him. He loved
her. Although he didn't deserve to have his prayer
answered, he begged for her to be all right.

He pleaded for the chance to tell her he loved her.

"Betsy Keene, small and mean." Clint Lockhart
smiled.

Betsy shivered, as much from that creepy smile as
his nasty little rhyme that he seemed to find so funny.
It was a fact that she was small; some folks called her
mousy. But she wasn't mean. She'd had a hard, lonely
time of it was all. Now it was her turn to have something or someone.

She'd thought her luck was changing when Clint
stumbled into her life months earlier. Men as handsome as sin didn't just fall off the turnip truck. But he
had done practically that. Only difference was, it was
a prison vehicle and he'd been wounded in the escape.
But that didn't matter since he'd been framed by the
Fortunes. Once he got even with Ryan Fortune, she
and Clint could finally be happy.

Only, she had to tell him she'd screwed up that
revenge.

She put her hand in the pocket of her worn jeans to
hide the shaking. It had been like that ever since she'd
fired off several shots at Matilda Fortune in the woods.
At Clint's insistence, she had followed the couple from
their house to the cabin.

Betsy closed her eyes at the memory. She still
couldn't believe what she'd done. Now she was even
more afraid. She had to tell Clint she'd failed to do as
he'd asked.

She lowered her gaze, but managed to lift her eyes
just enough to study him without his knowing. He was

just about the best-looking man she'd ever seen. His blue eyes and reddish-brown hair and six-feet-tall muscular body set her heart to fluttering something fierce. In her forty-odd years, no man had paid her any mind. She still couldn't hardly believe that a man like him could be interested in a nobody like her.

She was scared to death that he wouldn't give her the time of day when she told him she failed at the latest errand he'd sent her on. She'd been frightened to do it, but more afraid not to. Now she pictured her future without Clint in it, and didn't like what she saw. She had no one without him. Her folks were dead and her brother was on the run from the law. She hadn't seen or heard from him in years.

She'd tried her best to do whatever Clint told her to do. But when she'd pointed that gun, her hands had been shaking so. No way could she hit anything she aimed at. How in the world was she going to tell Clint and make him understand? More important, make him still love her?

"So, Sugar, don't keep me in suspense. Tell me what happened. Tell me how you got even with the Fortunes for me. I want to hear all of it, every last detail. Then I can leave this country a happy man. Just you and me, Sugar. You followed them, right? They didn't spot you, did they? Did she see you? Did she know what was coming? Was she afraid?"

She licked her dry lips. Suddenly her legs wouldn't hold her. She dropped into one of the gray vinyl dinette chairs. She felt as old and worn as the chair with the stuffing leaking out the back. As old and worn as the scratched metal cabinets in her tiny trailer. As ugly as the orange-and-gold sofa that Clint told her was the most godawful piece of furniture he'd ever seen.

"Clint, I—" she looked down at her fingers twisted together in her lap "—it's like this—"

He turned away, rubbing his hands together in glee. "It would have been better if Ryan could have seen her get it. Or if she'd died in a hospital with him at the bedside, with nothin' he could do to save her. That would've been the best. But he's got that ranch so tight with security, you couldn't have done it there."

"Clint you gotta listen—"

He whirled around, startling her. But the hardness in his blue eyes made her cold all over. "Spit it out, woman. You did take care of her like I asked? Right?"

She swallowed hard. "The gun you gave me—" Just a little white lie. What could it hurt? "It— It wasn't real accurate." The truth was, the Fortune woman had dropped before she'd fired. Then there wasn't a clear shot.

His handsome mouth twisted into an ugly grimace. "You didn't kill the Fortune bitch?"

"No. She was walking so fast. Sh-She was crying."

"Damn you, Betsy. If you went soft on me, so help me I'll make you regret the day you were born."

"I—I wouldn't do that, Clint. I love you."

"At least tell me you hit her. If she hurts, Ryan Fortune will hurt." The narrow-eyed look he leveled at her was cold, hard and ugly.

"You gotta understand, Clint. It wasn't easy. I— I'm not real good with guns."

"So she doesn't even have a scratch." Angrily, he brushed his arm across the kitchen table and sent newspapers, beer bottles and day-old dirty dishes flying.

Betsy jumped as they crashed to the floor, glass shattering. "I'm sorry, Clint. I can—"

"You can't do anything right, you cow. You're so stupid, you can't walk and chew gum at the same time. I don't know why I trusted you to do anything so important." His chest heaved from his outburst. He took a menacing step toward her. "How could I love a woman as dumb and ugly as you?"

"I'm sorry. Please don't be mad, Clint."

Fear clawed her insides. Not fear of Clint. Fear of being alone if he left her. The thought terrified. Maybe if she'd never met him… She had to think of something. She needed a plan that would put her back in his good graces. A way to get even with the Fortunes. The best way was through someone Ryan cared about. Someone he cared about who didn't live at the Double Crown. Betsy remembered the way Ryan had fawned over his godchild, Willa Simms. And she lived in College Station. And maybe there was a way no one had to die. Maybe just make the Fortunes worry. A kidnapping. She remembered a movie she'd seen where kidnappers demanded a whole pile of money. That just might work.

"I've got a better idea, Clint," she said. She licked her lips. "We can't get Matilda Fortune now because they'll be guarding her like Fort Knox."

"So?" There was a hint of curiosity in his expression.

"So, what if we kidnap that Willa Simms girl?"

"What the hell good will that do?" he asked, exasperated. He rested his hands on slim hips.

Betsy warmed to the idea when he continued to look at her. It was a good sign. "Think about it. We take her, and let Ryan stew for a spell. Then we send him a note and ask for a whole lot of money so's we'll give her back." She stood up and took a step forward, trying to think fast. To come up with details she knew would appeal to him.

Slowly, thoughtfully he nodded. "Betsy, you just might have something there. With Double Crown security so tight, I can't get to a Fortune. Next best thing is someone Ryan cares about. Not only can I get even with him, but he'll pay to get her back. And I'll have me some money. The ultimate revenge, let Ryan Fortune bankroll my new life when I hightail it outta here. It's perfect."

"The trick is to ask for enough. Then you can take me with you." She forced herself to meet his gaze, hoping she would see agreement.

Clint smiled the deadly smile that meant he approved. Whether it was the kidnap plan, or her suggestion to take her with him, Betsy wasn't sure.

He walked over to her and stroked her cheek with one finger, then lifted her chin with one knuckle of his fisted hand. He smiled down at her. "Sugar, I just might keep you around, after all."

Sixteen

"How many times do I have to tell you I'm fine?" Mattie shook her head in exasperation as she stared at a pacing Dawson. She sat in the middle of their big bed in San Antonio. He had fluffed the pillows behind her back more times than she could count. "The doctor at the ER said I'm fine. There's no need for you to hover over me like a mother hen."

Silently she prayed that he would ignore her token protest. She liked all the attention he'd showered on her. She was storing up the warm, fuzzy memories for the long lonely days and nights that stretched in front of her. Days and nights without Dawson.

He stopped pacing and met her gaze, the look in his eyes making her heart pound. *"Au contraire,"* he said. The side of the bed dipped as he sat beside her, his bent knee just an inch from her thigh. "There are several excellent reasons for me to hover. I left you once, and someone took a shot at you. If Clint Lockhart tries anything else, he'll have to go through me. He is not going to get near you again."

The expression on his face was intense, angry and pretty darn fierce, she thought, going all gooey inside.

She couldn't help smiling. "If he knows what's good for him, he should be afraid, very afraid. And if he comes anywhere near Kingston Estates—" she pointed at him "—one look at that face will send him running for cover."

"If he comes near you again, I'll take him apart." He never raised his voice, but threads of steel ran through it. She'd never heard that particular tone before.

She looked at him and tipped her head to the side as she committed his features to memory. The intense hazel eyes. Tense, square jaw. Muscular body. She decided what she would miss most was his wonderful smell. Her hero. Her husband. Hers for this moment only. How she wished she could stretch it into a lifetime.

"Still," she said hedging, "we don't know for sure that he was the one who shot at me."

Dawson slid her a wry look that shattered his worried expression just for an instant. "Who else could it be?" He held up his hand. "And don't give me your half-baked hunter theory. The cops dug a pistol slug out of that tree trunk. No self-respecting hunter would use a pistol. Not in Texas." He reached over and covered her cold hand with his warm one. "That bullet hit the tree right about where your head would have been. If you hadn't fainted—" He stopped and took a shuddering breath. "I don't even want to think about what would have happened. Which brings me to the other reason I feel the need to hover."

Knowing what was coming, she rolled her eyes. All the way home in the car he had asked every few minutes if she felt all right. Did she feel dizzy? Was she woozy? Was she awake? Maybe she shouldn't go to sleep. What if she had a concussion?

"I never faint," she said, heading off the barrage of questions. "In all the years I've worked with horses, I've had much worse injuries, and I have never passed out in my life.''

"Then how do you explain it? One second you were standing there, the next you dropped like a stone.''

That was the question of the day. Maybe her small drugstore purchase would give her the answer.

Dawson had insisted on bringing her home to San Antonio when the police finished questioning them. She had asked him to stop at a drugstore for something she desperately needed. She'd only managed to stop him from accompanying her when she claimed embarrassment at buying some feminine items in front of him. Besides, she'd told him, even if Clint had ambushed her, it was unlikely he was anywhere around. And certainly not inside that particular store. Even at that, Dawson had stood guard at the automatic doors, and didn't relax until she and he were barricaded inside the house. Before they'd even arrived, he'd been on the cell phone to Sheriff Wyatt Grayhawk and arranged for law enforcement around the home.

Home.

She sighed. How quickly she'd come to think of it that way, in spite of the fact that she knew very soon she would have to leave it. And Dawson. Tears burned at the backs of her eyes—a frequent occurrence of late. If it was hormones on account of—

She wouldn't go there. Not unless she had to. If she found out for sure that her fainting spell had happened for the reason she suspected, this marital situation could get a whole lot more complicated. Dawson's noble streak had gotten them into this situation in the first place. His mother-hen syndrome told her his heroic hat was still firmly in place. If he found out *this* news, he would never agree to a separation.

More than anything, she wanted to be his wife and grow old with him. She loved him, more than she'd thought possible. But she didn't want him to stay with her out of a misguided sense of duty. He'd been the one who told her everyone around an unhappy couple suffers—especially kids.

"Aren't you planning to go into the office today?" she asked, anxious for some privacy.

"Are you crazy?" He looked at her as if she were. "Now who needs to have their hearing checked? I just spent the last five minutes explaining why I feel the need to hover. I am not leaving you by yourself."

"But I'm fine—"

"I don't care," he interrupted. "I mean, of course I care. I'm glad you're fine. But I am not leaving this house, or you. Besides, Ryan gave me an executive order not to be at the office for a week. When I called him about what happened at the cabin, he reminded me of his order. You can't get rid of me, Mattie. I will not leave your side."

"Well, I'm going to have to leave yours," she said, sliding off the bed. As she did, their thighs brushed and she could almost see sparks, almost feel the flames of desire lick her from head to toe. More than anything, she wanted to be in his arms.

But she forced herself to keep going. *Practice,* she thought. She would need to remind herself every day without Dawson to just put one foot in front of the other.

She walked across the room and, without looking back at Dawson, shut the bathroom door between them.

Dawson had insisted Mattie rest all afternoon. Her color looked strange to him, her cheeks were white compared to the usual rose. He had taken the opportunity to make a few discreet phone calls. He'd been planning a surprise for Mattie. Partly to take her mind off the danger surrounding her, but mostly because he'd been given another chance and he wasn't about to blow it. He just needed to set the stage.

While Mattie slept, he'd set up a table in front of the fireplace. He'd used candles, crystal and china. Nothing but the best for his bride. That meant he needed help with food. He'd called a restaurant in town and ordered dinner, which had been delivered a few minutes earlier. Now all he needed was Mattie.

He knew she would always be all he needed. If his luck held, he would find the right combination of words to convince her of that.

As if on cue, she walked into the kitchen, sleepily rubbing her eyes. His heart started to pound at the sight of her—silky strands of blond hair tousled from sleep, sweatpants hugging her luscious curves, T-shirt pulled tight across her breasts. He ached with need for her.

She yawned. "Who's coming to dinner?" she asked, sniffing the delicious aromas while looking around at all the preparations.

"I hope you are."

Suddenly the drowsiness vanished, replaced by wariness. "You did all this for me?"

"I did. Now go sit down by the fire where it's warm. I'll bring dinner in."

"Okay," she said in a voice that told him she didn't trust everything not to disappear.

Dawson fixed two plates—lasagna, salad, garlic bread. He tucked a bottle of Merlot under his arm and took everything into the family room. Mattie sat there in front of a roaring fire, the flames' glow turning her hair to burnished gold. She had never looked more beautiful to him.

He set the plates down then opened the wine and poured them each a glass. He picked his up. "Let's drink to second chances," he said.

She hesitated a moment before picking up her glass. "Whatever you say," she answered.

When she didn't drink, Dawson was afraid his come-to-realize had come too late. Still, there were a few things he had to get off his chest.

Dawson put his glass down and covered her hand with his own. "Mattie, there's something I have to tell you." She stared at him and he knew she was listening intently. He took a deep breath. "You didn't let me finish what I was saying in the cabin."

"When?" she asked, her brow wrinkling.

"I told you my parents were mismatched, and in your usual impetuous, wonderful way you jumped to the wrong conclusion."

"Okay. Then tell me the right conclusion."

"My mother shared with me something that she discovered about her and my father. She said when you find the great love of your life, don't let go. Don't let pride or anything else tear you apart."

"But you said they were wrong for each other. That she demanded more time than he had to give."

He nodded and nervously twirled his wineglass. "She found out too late that she would have been happier with the small amount of time he could give than not having him at all. She told me not to make the same mistake."

Mattie's gaze narrowed on him. "What are you trying to say?"

He drew in a deep breath as he rubbed his jaw. "When I heard that gunshot and found you on the ground—" He shook his head. "I've never been so afraid in my life. I thought I'd lost you. My life flashed before my eyes—a life without you—and it was worse than anything I could imagine." He shook his head. "No, only one thing would have been worse—not telling you how I feel."

She turned her hand palm up and linked her fingers with his. "Tell me now, Dawson. How do you feel?"

"I love you, Matilda Theodora Fortune Prescott." The words came out easily, after all.

Her eyes widened. "You picked a good time to call me that. I'm too stunned to retaliate."

"It's true. I fell in love with you the first time I set eyes on you, I just didn't know it. I love your spirit and your courage. Not a day will go by for the rest of our lives that you won't know how very glad I am that you're mine. I want to grow old with you." He laughed. "Older than I am now, anyway. I want to have children with you. As soon as possible. I'm not getting any younger."

Mattie stared at him. She blinked three times to make sure she wasn't dreaming. He had just said he loved her. Who knew that out of something so violent and frightening, a fantasy so wonderful and beautiful could come true?

"If I'd known it would take getting shot at to bring you around, I'd have done it sooner," she joked. "I have something—"

"That's not funny." He scowled.

"Lighten up, Dawson. Don't you see? I love you, too. You need to know—"

"Then why didn't you drink to second chances?" he asked, staring at her untouched wineglass. "If we're okay, it's customary to drink to the toast."

"That's what I'm trying to tell you." She squeezed his hand. "It's about all those children you want. I think we…got a jump start. It could be sooner than you thought."

He stared at her for a moment, then a slow, sexy, wonderful smile turned up the corners of his mouth. "Are you saying what I think you are?"

He actually looked happy. *Life just doesn't get any better than this,* she thought, grinning back. She nodded. "Why do you think I made you stop at the drugstore?"

"So the female stuff was a pregnancy test? You should have told me."

"I didn't want to say anything until I was sure. But I've been feeling sort of sick for the last few days. And when I fainted—" She stopped, realizing the magnitude of it all.

"The baby saved your life," he said, putting her thoughts into words. He was beside her in a heartbeat, down on one knee with his hand gently, protectively covering her abdomen. "This tiny miraculous result of our love actually saved your life—" His voice cracked. "I can't believe you were talking about a divorce."

"It was all that respect malarkey. I thought it was your way of saying you could never love me."

"You were wrong. I was just afraid to tell you I love you. Big difference."

She covered his hand with her own as together they

protected their child. "I can't wait to meet your mom. She's a very wise woman, and I think I'm going to like her very much."

"And she's going to love you. She'll be thrilled about becoming a grandmother." He reached into his pocket and pulled out a velvet jeweler's box.

Mattie's smile grew wider. It was a small box—the best kind. "Is that what I think it is?"

"You one-upped me with the news about the baby. But I'd planned to do this, and I learned the hard way that there's no time like the present." He opened the box, then lifted her left hand and slipped on a diamond engagement ring. "This ring was my grandmother's. It symbolizes to me that love has no beginning and no end. It's as strong and precious as the diamond at its center. For a methodical man, I've managed to do everything backward—mating, marriage, courtship. This proposal is a little backward and a bit late, but the sentiment is heartfelt and sincere. Will you be my wife?"

"Yes. I had just about given up on my fairy tale." She grinned down at him—the wavery him that she saw through tears of happiness. "I don't just mean the bent-knee proposal. All I've ever wanted is a loving relationship and children. You've given me both. Without a doubt, I am the happiest woman on earth. I love you with all my heart, husband."

"I love you more, wife."

"I plan to spend every day for the rest of my life making you happy. Here's a sample." Mattie leaned down and kissed him. She pulled back and smiled. "That first time in your arms was a night I'll never forget."

"Do you want to thank Griff, or should I?" he asked.

She laughed. "Thanks hardly seem adequate considering what he gave us. It was a very special night."

He stood and pulled her to her feet. "There are more where that came from."

"I'm counting on it."

Arms around each other, they walked down the hall to their bedroom. Mattie's heart was so full of happiness she felt it wouldn't hold any more. She was the luckiest woman in the world. One night of beauty had made all her dreams come true.

* * * * *

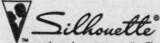

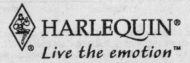

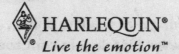

"Joanna Wayne weaves together a romance and suspense
with pulse-pounding results!"
—*New York Times* bestselling author Tess Gerritsen

National bestselling author

JOANNA WAYNE

Alligator Moon

Determined to find his brother's killer, John Robicheaux finds
himself entangled with investigative reporter Callie Havelin.
Together they must shadow the sinister killer slithering in the
murky waters—before they are consumed by the darkness....

A riveting tale that shouldn't be missed!

Coming in June 2004.

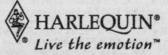

Coming in May 2004 to Silhouette Books

When Jake Ingram is taken captive by the Coalition, a sexy undercover agent is sent to brainwash him. Though he finds her hard to resist, can he trust this mysterious beauty?

Five extraordinary siblings.

One dangerous past.

Unlimited potential.

Look for more titles in this exhilarating new series, available only from Silhouette Books.